Applying Use Case
Driven Object
Modeling with UML

D1307838

Applying Use Case Driven Object Modeling with UML

An Annotated e-Commerce Example

Doug Rosenberg and Kendall Scott

ADDISON-WESLEY

Boston • San Francisco • New York • Totonto
Montreal • London • Munich • Paris • Madrid
Capetown • Sydney • Tokyo • Singapore • Mexico City

The publisher offers discounts on this book when ordered in quantity for special sales. For more information, please contact:

Pearson Education Corporate Sales Division
One Lake Street
Upper Saddle River, NJ 07458
(800) 382-3419
corpsales@pearsontechgroup.com

Visit us on the Web at www.awl.com/cseng/.

Library of Congress Cataloging-in-Publication Data

Rosenberg, Doug.
    Applying use case driven object modeling with UML: an annotated e-commerce
example / Doug Rosenberg, Kendall Scott.
        p. cm.
    ISBN 0-201-73039-1
    1. Object-oriented methods (Computer science)   2. UML (Computer science)   3. Use
cases (systems engineering)   4. E-commerce.   I. Scott, Kendall, 1960-   II. Title.

QA76.9.O35 R63 2001
005.1'17—dc21

2001034319

ISBN 0-201-73039-1
Text printed on recycled and acid-free paper
1 2 3 4 5 6 7 8 9–CRW–05 04 03 02 01
First printing, June 2001

We dedicate this book to the memory of Tom Johnson,
whose steady and dependable work kept both of us busy teaching
the training workshops that gave us the source material for this book.
Tom's untimely passing as the manuscript was in final
production saddened all of us who knew him.
He will be sorely missed.

Contents

Figures

Preface

Theory, in Practice

In our first book, *Use Case Driven Object Modeling with UML*, we suggested that the difference between theory and practice was that in theory, there is no difference between theory and practice, but in practice, there is. In that book, we attempted to reduce OOAD modeling theory to a practical subset that was easy to learn and pretty much universally applicable, based on our experience in teaching this material to people working on hundreds of projects since about 1993.

Now, two years after hitting the shelves, that book is in its fifth printing. But even though our work has been favorably received, it seems like the job isn't all the way done yet. "We need to see more use case and UML modeling examples" is a phrase we've been hearing fairly often over the last couple of years. And, as we've used the first book as the backbone of training workshops where we apply the theory to real client projects, it has become clear that the process of reviewing the models is critically important and not well understood by many folks.

So, although we present a fairly extensive example in our first book, we convinced Addison-Wesley to let us produce this companion workbook, in which we dissect the design of an Internet bookstore, step-by-step, in great detail. This involves showing many common mistakes, and then showing the relevant pieces of the model with their mistakes corrected. We chose an Internet bookstore because it's relevant to many of today's projects in the Web-driven world, and because we've been teaching workshops using this example and, as a result, had a rich source of classroom UML models with real student mistakes in them.

We collected some of our favorite mistakes—that is, the kind of mistakes we saw getting repeated over and over again—and built this workbook around those models. And then we added three new chapters about reviews—one on requirements reviews, one on preliminary design reviews, and one on critical design reviews.

What really makes this book unique, though, is the fact that you, the reader, get to correct the mistakes.

The Premise

After we give you an overview of the ICONIX process in Chapter 1, four of the seven subsequent chapters address the four key phases of the process in some detail. The format of each of these chapters is as follows:

- The first part describes the essence of domain modeling (Chapter 2), use case modeling (Chapter 3), robustness analysis (Chapter 5), or sequence diagrams (Chapter 7), and places the material in the context of the "big picture" of the process. In each of these chapters, you'll work through pieces of the Internet bookstore example, and then you'll see an overview diagram at the end of the chapter that brings the relevant pieces together. We present fragments of ten different use cases in Chapter 3; we carry five of these forward through preliminary design and detailed design in Chapters 5 and 7, respectively. (The fragments of class diagrams that appear in Chapter 2 also trace into the use case text and to full class diagrams that appear in Chapters 5 and 7.)

- The next section describes the key elements of the given phase. Each of these sections is basically a condensed version of an associated chapter in *Use Case Driven Object Modeling with UML*, with some new information added within each chapter.

- The following section describes the top 10 mistakes that our students tend to make during workshops in which we teach the process. We've added five new Top 10 lists in this book: Top 10 robustness analysis errors, Top 10 sequence diagramming errors, and Top 10 mistakes to avoid for each of the three "review" chapters.

- The final section presents a set of five exercises for you to work, to test your knowledge of the material in the chapter.

The following aspects are common to each set of exercises:

- There's a red box, with a white label, at the top of each right-hand page. For the domain modeling and use case exercises, this label takes the form Exercise X; for the robustness analysis and sequence diagram exercises, the label takes the form of a use case name. (We'll explain the significance of this soon.)

- There are three or four mistakes on each right-hand page. Each mistake has a "Top 10" logo next to it that indicates which rule is being violated.

- The left-hand page on the flip side of each "red" page has a black box, with a white label, at the top. Corrections to the errors presented on the associated "bad" page are explicitly indicated; explanations of the mistakes appear at the bottom of the page.

Your task is to write corrections on each "bad" exercise page *before* you flip it over to see the "good" exercise diagram.

To summarize: Chapter 2 presents classes used by the ten sample use cases. Chapter 3 presents fragments from all of those use cases. Chapters 5 and 7 present diagrams connected with five of the use cases. The idea is that you'll move from a partial understanding of the use cases through to sequence diagrams that present full text, and some of the associated elements of the detailed design, for each use case.

What about the other three chapters, you ask?

- Chapter 4 describes how to perform requirements review, which involves trying to ensure that the use cases and the domain model work together to address the customers' functional requirements.

- Chapter 6 describes how to perform preliminary design review (PDR), which involves trying to ensure that robustness diagrams exist for all use cases (and are consistent with those use cases), the domain model has a fairly rich set of attributes that correspond well with whatever prototypes are in place (and all of the objects needed by the use cases are represented in that model), and the development team is ready to move to detailed design.

- Chapter 8 describes how to perform critical design review (CDR), which involves trying to ensure that the "how" of detailed design, as shown on sequence diagrams, matches up well with the "what" that the use cases specify, and that the detailed design is of sufficient depth to facilitate a relatively small and seamless leap into code.

All three of these review chapters offer overviews, details, and top 10 lists, but we don't make you work any more exercises. What these reviews have in common is the goal of ensuring consistency of the various parts of the model, as expressed on the "good" exercise diagrams.

The Appendix contains a report that summarizes the model for the bookstore; you can download the full model from **http://www.iconixsw.com/WorkbookExample.html**. The Appendix contains all of the diagrams that appear in the body of the book, but the full model includes design details for the other five use cases. This allows you to go through these use cases as further exercises, and then compare your results to ours; we highly recommend that you do this.

Cool premise, isn't it? We're not aware of another book like this one, and we're hoping you'll find it useful in your efforts to apply use case driven object modeling with UML.

Acknowledgments

Doug would like to thank his intrepid crew at ICONIX, especially Andrea Lee for her work on the script for the Inside the ICONIX Process CD, which we borrowed heavily from for Chapter 1, along with Chris Starczak, Jeff Kantor, and Erin Arnold. Doug would also like to thank Kendall for (finally) agreeing that yes, this *would* make the book better, and yes, we *do* have time to add that, and yes, the fact that R comes before S *does* mean that Mr. Rosenberg has more votes than Mr. Scott. [Co-author's note to self: Get name legally changed to Scott Kendall before the next book comes out. *That'll* teach him.]

Doug and Kendall would like to thank Paul Becker and all the fine folks at Addison-Wesley (including Ross Venables, who's no longer there but who got this project off the ground) who somehow managed to compress the production schedule to compensate for the delays in the writing schedule (which are all Kendall's fault). We'd also like to thank the reviewers of the manuscript, especially Mark Woodbury, whose incisive comments about "defragmenting" the example gave us the push we needed to get it the point where we think it's really, really cool as opposed to just really cool. And, we'd like to thank Greg Wilson, who reviewed our first book for *Dr. Dobbs' Journal*, liked it, and suggested that we write a companion workbook. Specifically, he said: "The second criticism of this book is one that I thought I'd never make: It is simply too short. Having finally found a useful, readable, and practical description of a design-centered development methodology, I really wanted a dozen or more examples of each point to work through. If the authors were to produce a companion workbook, I can promise them that they'd have at least one buyer."

Finally, Kendall would like to thank Doug for raising the art of snarkiness to a level that makes Kendall look like a paragon of good cheer in comparison to Doug.

Doug Rosenberg
Santa Monica, California
May 2001
dougr@iconixsw.com
http://www.iconixsw.com

Kendall Scott
Harrison, Tennessee
May 2001
kendall@usecasedriven.com
http://www.usecasedriven.com

Chapter 1

Introduction

The ICONIX process sits somewhere in between the very large Rational Unified Process (RUP) and the very small eXtreme programming approach (XP). The ICONIX process is use case driven, like the RUP, but without a lot of the overhead that the RUP brings to the table. It's also relatively small and tight, like XP, but it doesn't discard analysis and design like XP does. This process also makes streamlined use of the Unified Modeling Language (UML) while keeping a sharp focus on the traceability of requirements. And, the process stays true to Ivar Jacobson's original vision of what "use case driven" means, in that it results in concrete, specific, readily understandable use cases that a project team can actually use to drive the development effort.

The approach we follow takes the best of three methodologies that came into existence in the early 1990s. These methodologies were developed by the folks that now call themselves the "three amigos": Ivar Jacobson, Jim Rumbaugh, and Grady Booch. We use a subset of the UML, based on Doug's analysis of the three individual methodologies.

There's a quote in Chapter 32 of *The Unified Modeling Language User Guide*, written by the amigos, that says, "You can model 80 percent of most problems by using about 20 percent of the UML." However, nowhere in this book do the authors tell you which 20 percent that might be. Our subset of the UML focuses on the core set of notations that you'll need to do most of your modeling work. Within this workbook we also explain how you can use other elements of the UML and where to add them as needed.

One of our favorite quotes is, "The difference between theory and practice is that in theory, there is no difference between theory and practice, but in practice, there is." In practice, there never seems to be enough time to do modeling, analysis, and design. There's always pressure from management to jump to code, to start coding prematurely because progress on software projects tends to get measured by how much code exists. Our approach is a minimalist, streamlined approach that focuses on that area that lies in between use cases and code. Its emphasis is on what needs to happen at that point in the life cycle where you're starting out: you have a start on some use cases, and now you need to do a good analysis and design.

Our goal has been to identify a minimal yet sufficient subset of the UML (and of modeling in general) that seems generally to be necessary in order to do a good job on your software project. We've been refining our definition of "minimal yet sufficient" in this context for eight or nine years now. The approach we're telling you about in this workbook is one that has been used on hundreds of projects and has been proven to work reliably across a wide range of industries and project situations.

A Walk (Backwards) through the ICONIX Process

Figure 1-1 shows the key question that the ICONIX process aims to answer.

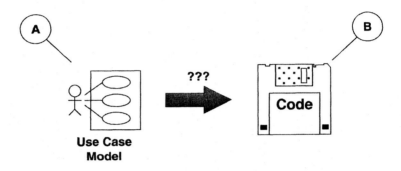

How do we get from use cases to code?

Figure 1-1: *Use Cases to Code*

What we're going to illustrate is how to get from point A to point B directly, in the shortest possible time. (Actually, we're not going to go all the way to code, but we'll take you close enough so you can taste it.) You can think of point A as representing this thought: "I have an idea of what my system has to do, and I have a start on some use cases," and point B as representing some completed, tested, debugged code that actually does what the use cases said it needed to do. In other words, the code implements the required behavior, as defined by the use cases. This book focuses on how we can get you from the fuzzy, nebulous area of "I think I want it to do something like this" to making those descriptions unambiguous, complete, and rigorous, so you can produce a good, solid architecture, a robust software design, then (by extension) nice clean code that actually implements the behavior that your users want.

We're going to work backwards from code and explain the steps to our goal. We'll explain why we think the set of steps we're going to teach is the minimal set of steps you need, yet is sufficient for most cases in closing the gap between use cases and code. Figure 1-2 shows the three assumptions we're going to make to start things off: that we've done some prototyping; that we have made some idea of what our user interface might look like; and that we might have some start in identifying the scenarios or use cases in our system.

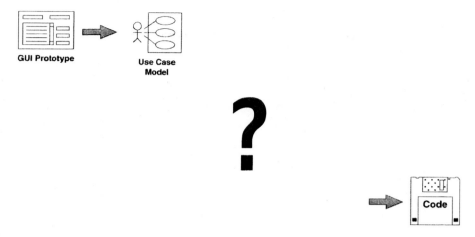

Figure 1-2: *Starting Off*

This puts us at the point where we're about to launch into analysis and design. What we want to find out is how we can get from this starting point to code. When we begin, there's only a big question mark—we have some nebulous, fuzzy ideas of what our system has to do, and we need to close this gap before we start coding.

In object-oriented systems, the structure of our code is defined by classes. So, before we write code, we'd like to know what our software classes are going to be. To do this, we need one or more class diagrams that show the classes in the system. On each of these classes, we need a complete set of attributes, which are the data members contained in the classes, and operations, which define what the software functions are. In other words, we need to have all our software functions identified, and we need to make sure we have the data those functions require to do their job.

We'll need to show how those classes encapsulate that data and those functions. We show how our classes are organized and how they relate to each other on class diagrams. We'll use the UML class diagram as the vehicle to display this information. Ultimately, what we want to get to is a set of very detailed design-level class diagrams. By **design-level**, we mean a level of detail where the class diagram is very much a template for the actual code of the system—it shows exactly how your code is going to be organized.

Figure 1-3 shows that class diagrams are the step before code, and there is a design-level diagram that maps one-to-one from classes on your diagram to classes in your source code. But there's still a gap. Instead of going from use cases to code, now we need to get from use cases to design-level class diagrams.

One of the hardest things to do in object-oriented software development is **behavior allocation**, which involves making decisions for every software function that you're going to build. For each function, you have to decide which class in your software design should be the class that contains it. We need to allocate all the behavior of the system—every software function needs to be allocated into the set of classes that we're designing.

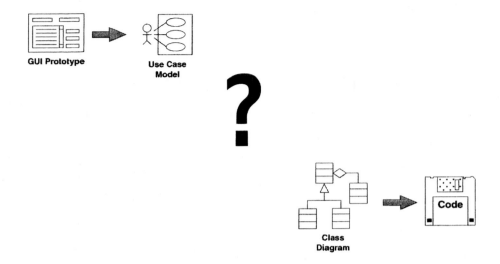

Figure 1-3: *Class Diagrams Map Out the Structure of the Code*

One UML diagram that's extremely useful in this area is the sequence diagram. This diagram is an ideal vehicle to help you make these behavior allocation decisions. Sequence diagrams are done on a per-scenario basis: for every scenario in our system, we'll draw a sequence diagram that shows us which object is responsible for which function in our code. The sequence diagram shows how runtime object instances communicate by passing messages. Each message invokes a software function on the object that receives the message. This is why it's an ideal diagram for visualizing behavior allocation.

Figure 1-4 shows that the gap between use cases and code is getting smaller as we continue to work backwards. Now, we need to get from use cases to sequence diagrams.

We'll make our decisions about allocating behavior to our classes as we draw the sequence diagrams. That's going to put the operations on the software classes. When you use a visual modeling tool such as Rational Rose or GDPro, as you draw the message arrows on the sequence diagrams, you're actually physically assigning operations to the classes on the class diagrams. The tool enforces the fact that behavior allocation happens from the sequence diagram. As you're drawing the sequence diagram, the classes on the class diagram get populated with operations.

So, the trick is to get from use cases to sequence diagrams. This is a non-trivial problem in most cases because the use cases present a requirements-level view of the system, and the sequence diagram is a very detailed design view. This is where our approach is different from the other approaches on the market today. Most approaches talk about use cases and sequence diagrams but don't address how to get across the gap between the fuzzy use cases and a code-like level of detail on the sequence diagrams. Getting across this gap between *what* and *how* is the central aspect of the ICONIX process.

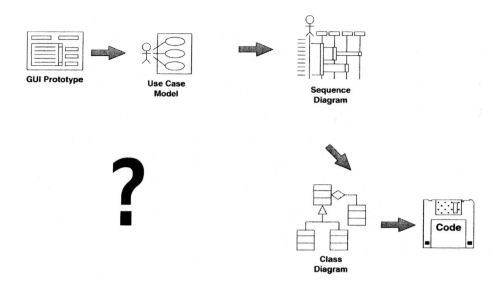

Figure 1-4: *Sequence Diagrams Help Us Allocate Operations (Behavior) to Classes*

What we're going to do now is close the gap between the fuzzy, nebulous use case and the very detailed and precise sequence diagram with another kind of diagram called a **robustness diagram**. The robustness diagram sits in the gap between requirements and detailed design; it will help make getting from the use cases to the sequence diagrams easier.

If you've been looking at UML literature, the robustness diagram was originally only partially included in the UML. It originated in Ivar Jacobson's work and got included in the UML standard as an appendage. This has to do with the history and the sequence of how Booch, Rumbaugh, and Jacobson got together and merged their methodologies, as opposed to the relative importance of the diagram in modeling.

Across the top of a sequence diagram is a set of objects that are going to be participating in a given scenario. One of the things we have to do before we can get to a sequence diagram is to have a first guess as to which objects will be participating in that scenario. It also helps if we have a guess as to what software functions we'll be performing in the scenario. While we do the sequence diagram, we'll be thinking about mapping the set of functions that will accomplish the desired behavior onto that set of objects that participate in the scenario.

It helps a great deal to have a good idea about the objects that we'll need and the functions that those objects will need to perform. When you do it the second time, it's a lot more accurate than when you take a first guess at it. The process that we're following, which is essentially Ivar Jacobson's process as described in his Objectory work, is a process that incorporates a first guess, or preliminary design, the results of which appear on what we call a robustness diagram. We refine that first guess into a detailed design on the sequence diagram. So, we'll do a sequence diagram for each scenario that we're going to build.

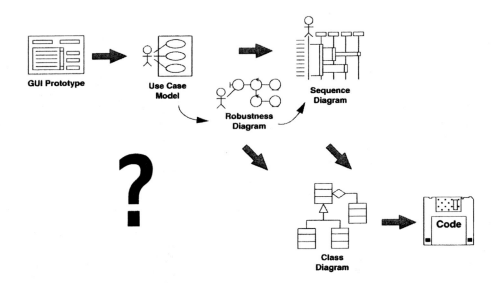

Figure 1-5: *Robustness Diagrams Close the Gap Between Requirements and Detailed Design*

Figure 1-5 shows that we're adding a diagram to our subset of UML. The robustness diagram was described in the original UML specs, but its definition was in an extra document called *Objectory Process-Specific Extensions*. What we've found over the past ten years is that it's very difficult to get from use cases to sequence diagrams without this technique. Using the robustness diagram helps avoid the common problem of project teams thrashing around with use cases and not really getting anywhere towards their software design. If you incorporate this step, it will make this process and your project much easier. We didn't invent robustness analysis, but we're trying to make sure it doesn't get forgotten. Robustness analysis has proven to be an invaluable aid in getting across the gap between requirements and design.

Robustness analysis sits right in the gap between what the system has to do and how it's actually going to accomplish this task. While we're crossing this gap, there are actually several different activities that are going on concurrently. First, we're going to be discovering objects that we forgot when we took our first guess at what objects we had in the system. We can also add the attributes onto our classes as we trace data flow on the robustness diagrams. Another important thing we'll do is update and refine the text of the use case as we work through this diagram.

We still have a question mark, though. That question mark relates to the comment we just made about discovering the objects that we forgot when we took our first guess. This implies that we're going to take a first guess at some point.

There's a magic phrase that we use to help teach people how to write use cases successfully: *Describe system usage in the context of the object model*. The first thing this means is that we're not talking, in this book, about writing fuzzy, abstract and vague, ambiguous use cases that don't have enough detail in them from which to produce a software design. We're going to teach you to write use cases that are very explicit, precise, and unambiguous. We have a very specific goal in mind when discussing use cases: we want to drive the software design from them. Many books on use cases take a different perspective, using use cases as more of an abstract requirements exploration technique. Our approach is different because our goals are different. Remember, our mission is to help you get from use cases to code.

We'll start out with something called a domain model, which is a kind of glossary of the main abstractions—in other words, the most important nouns that are in our problem space (our problem domain). In the term **domain model**, the word "domain" comes from the idea of the problem domain. For example, if our problem domain is electronic commerce—as it is in the workbook, amazingly enough—we'll probably have a domain object like a catalog or a purchase order. We're going to call these nouns that belong to our problem space **domain objects**, and we're going to produce, at the very beginning of our analysis and design activities, something called a domain model, which lays all these domain objects out on one big UML class diagram.

On our robustness diagrams, we're also going to use something called **boundary objects**. Among the boundary objects, we find things like the screens of the system. In the text of our use cases, we want to explicitly reference both domain objects and boundary objects. We'll write about such things as how the users interact with the screens and how those screens interact with the domain objects, which often have some mapping onto a database that may sit behind the OO part of our system. Our use case text will get a lot more specific and a lot less ambiguous if we follow this guideline of describing how the system is used in the context of the object model as it evolves.

During domain modeling, we want to identify the most important set of abstractions that describe the problem space, or the problem domain of the system, that we need to build. For this task, we'll follow the methodology Jim Rumbaugh developed: the Object Modeling Technique (OMT), which is a very thorough treatment of some useful techniques for helping us do this domain model.

One difference between our approach and some of the other use case–oriented approaches you might run across is that we insist on starting the whole process with domain modeling. In writing our use cases against the set of nouns in the domain model, thus using that domain model as a glossary, we can unambiguously define a set of terms that we can reference within our use case text. This approach proves to be quite useful, especially when you're working in a team environment where there are multiple groups of people that are trying to describe scenarios in different parts of the system. If you get closure and agreement on what the important nouns in the system are, you eliminate whole layers of ambiguity in the use case models. For example, this enables you to be clear on what a purchase order is, what a line item is, and what a shopping cart is. All those things are clear from the beginning, due to the fact that we've defined a glossary of terms before we start writing our use cases.

In terms of the UML, the domain model is basically a class diagram, so it's the same kind of diagram as our design-level class diagram. Generally, on the domain model, we suppress quite a bit of detail; in particular, we don't show the attributes and the operations on the classes. The domain model is more of a global summary-level class diagram. In fact, it's a first guess at a class diagram, focusing entirely on the problem domain of the system we're building. We take this first guess at our class diagram, and then we work through all the details of our use cases and refine our view of the system. As we work through the scenarios, the first-guess class diagram evolves into our detailed static model for the system.

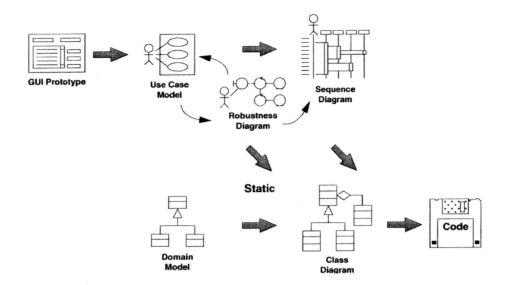

Figure 1-6: *Referencing Domain Objects by Name Removes Ambiguity from the Use Cases*

As you can see in Figure 1-6, we now have a fairly complete picture, with no big gaps in it, that helps us get from use cases and prototypes over on the left side to design-level class diagrams and source code over on the right side.

Note that we're using a very streamlined approach. We're only using four different kinds of UML diagrams. That's four out of a set of nine different kinds of diagrams that make up the UML. Generally, for most projects, most of the time you can do most of your work using less than half of the UML. Limiting your focus to this core subset of diagrams will make a significant impact on your learning curve as you learn how to do modeling with UML.

We're going to start off with the domain model, which is an analysis-level class diagram, as our first guess at the static structure of the system. We're going to continuously refine and add detail to this model, with the ultimate result being our detailed design. The class diagram, which is in the bottom half of Figure 1-6, is a static description of how the code is organized, whereas the use cases are a dynamic description of the runtime behavior.

We'll take the first guess at our static model, and then we'll spend most of our time working through use case after use case. Every time we work through a use case, we'll add some detail to the class diagram. After we work through all the scenarios that the system has to support, add in all the detail needed to make all those scenarios happen, and review what we've done a couple of times, we should have a design that meets the requirements, and we'll be well positioned to write code.

Figure 1-7 shows the "big picture" for the ICONIX process. This figure appears on the first page of every chapter in our book *Use Case Driven Object Modeling with UML*. The picture has two parts to it: The top part is the dynamic model, which describes behavior, and the bottom part is the static model, which describes structure.

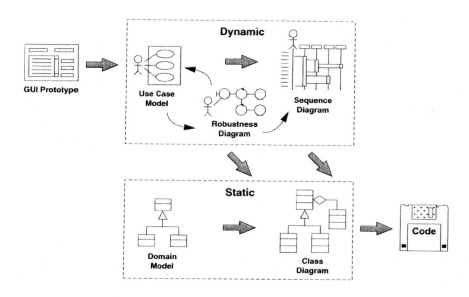

Figure 1-7: *The ICONIX Process—A Streamlined Approach to UML Modeling*

We might start with some prototypes, or perhaps simple line drawings of our screens. Then, after getting some assurance from users that we're on the right track, we can work from this beginning to identify use cases on our use case diagram, which shows all the scenarios that the system has to perform. Then we write the text of our use cases. We refine the use case text during robustness analysis. It's important to try to get the text stabilized and corrected during the preliminary design phase before moving into detailed design, which we do on sequence diagrams.

Many people complain about constantly changing requirements. Some use this as an excuse to start coding prematurely. We're willing to bet that the vast majority of these folks have never used robustness analysis, which is enormously helpful in getting those requirements stabilized.

By breaking exploration of the dynamic model into these three steps, we get two chances to review the behavior description; hopefully, by the time we've reviewed it the second time, our understanding of the required behavior is detailed and fairly stable, and we can start designing against it.

As you can see on the static part of the picture, we start with a quick first guess about objects based totally on the problem space description. We go through one long continuous refinement that's driven by our analysis of the dynamic runtime behavior of the system. We think in detail how one scenario is supposed to work, then update our class diagrams based on our improved understanding of that. Then, we go back and think more about what the behavior of the system should be.

Next, we refine our software structure accordingly. Our approach, which is derived 80 percent from Ivar Jacobson's work, is a very natural way to decompose systems along use case boundaries, and then use the results of the use case analysis to drive the object modeling forward to a level that's detailed enough to code from.

Key Features of the ICONIX Process

Figure 1-7 shows the essence of a *streamlined* approach to software development that includes a minimal set of UML diagrams, and some valuable techniques, that you can use to get from use cases to code *quickly* and *efficiently*. The approach is flexible and open; you can always elect to use other aspects of the UML to supplement the basic materials.

We'd like to point out three significant features of this approach.

First, the approach offers *streamlined usage of the UML*. The steps that we describe in the upcoming chapters represent a "minimalist" approach—they comprise the minimal set of steps that we've found to be necessary and sufficient on the road to a successful OO development project. By focusing on a subset of the large and often unwieldy UML, a project team can also head off "analysis paralysis" at the pass.

Second, the approach offers a high degree of *traceability*. At every step along the way, you refer back to the requirements in some way. There is never a point at which the process allows you to stray too far from the user's needs. Traceability also refers to the fact that you can track objects from step to step, as well, as analysis melds into design.

Third, the approach is *iterative* and *incremental*, although we might not be using these terms in the traditional sense. Multiple iterations occur between developing the domain model and identifying and analyzing the use cases. Other iterations exist, as well, as the team proceeds through the life cycle. The static model gets refined incrementally during the successive iterations through the dynamic model (composed of use cases, robustness analysis, and sequence diagrams). Please note, though, that the approach doesn't require formal milestones and a lot of bookkeeping; rather, the refinement efforts result in natural milestones as the project team gains knowledge and experience.

As we described in the Preface, we're going to demonstrate these aspects of the ICONIX process in the context of an on-line bookstore; the focus will be on the customer's view of the system.

The fact that we've been able to teach this process, with only minimal changes, over an entire decade, with it remaining useful and relevant today, is made possible because our process is based on finding the answers to some fundamentally important questions about a system. These questions include the following:

- Who are the users of the system (the actors), and what are they trying to do?
- What are the "real world" (problem domain) objects and the associations among them?
- What objects are needed for each use case?
- How do the objects collaborating within each use case interact?
- How will we handle real-time control issues?
- How are we really going to build this system on a nuts-and-bolts level?

We have yet to come across a system that doesn't need to have these basic questions answered (especially the first four questions), or one that couldn't use the techniques described in this book to help answer them using an iterative, incremental, opportunistic (when you see the answer, capture it) approach. Although the full approach presents the steps in a specific order, it's not crucial that you follow the steps in that order. Many a project has died a horrible death because of a heavy, restrictive, overly prescriptive "cement collar" process, and we are by no means proponents of this approach. What we are saying is that *missing answers to any of these questions will add a significant amount of risk to a development effort.*

Process Fundamentals

We believe that the best way to make process more attractive is to educate as many people as possible about the benefits of answering the questions we raised earlier, along with similar questions, and about the risks of failing to answer them. Building good object models is straightforward *if you keep ruthlessly focused on answering the fundamentally important questions about the system you are building and refuse to get caught up in superfluous modeling issues.* That philosophy lies at the heart of the ICONIX process.

The people who have to use the process, and management, are both customers of a software development process. We think of a process as a road map for a team to follow, a map that identifies a set of landmarks, or **milestones**, along the way to producing a quality product.

There are various paths a team can travel, depending on the capabilities and preferences of its members. But no matter which path they go down, at some point, they must reach the milestones. At these points in the process, their work becomes visible to management—during reviews of intermediate results. Passing the milestones does not guarantee a quality product, but it should greatly improve the chances.

We believe milestones for an object-oriented process should include, at a minimum, the following.

- The team has identified and described all the usage scenarios for the system it's about to build.
- The team has taken a hard look for reusable abstractions (classes) that participate in multiple scenarios.
- The team has thought about the problem domain and has identified classes that belong to that domain—in other words, the team has thought about reusability beyond just this system.
- The team has verified that all functional requirements of the system are accounted for in the design.
- The team has thought carefully about how the required system behavior gets allocated to the identified abstractions, taking into consideration good design principles such as minimizing coupling, maximizing cohesion, generality, and sufficiency, and so forth.

Beyond these milestones, there are at least four other fundamental requirements of a process.

1. It has to be flexible enough to accommodate different styles and kinds of problems.
2. It has to support the way people really work (including prototyping and iterative/incremental development).
3. It needs to serve as a guide for less-experienced members of the team, helping them be as productive as possible without handcuffing more experienced members.
4. It needs to expose the precode products of a development effort to management in a reasonably standard and comprehensible form.

The Process in a Nutshell

The basic steps that comprise the full ICONIX process and the associated milestones are presented in Figures 1-8 to 1-11. Note that the first three of these diagrams will appear again later in the text, to remind you where we are in the overall process. (We don't talk about implementation in this book, but we do have a chapter about implementation in the original book. Figure 1-11 is here for completeness.)

These diagrams together illustrate three key principles that underlie the process: inside-out, outside-in, and top-down, all at the same time.

1. Work inward from the user requirements.

2. Work outward from the key abstractions of the problem domain.

3. Drill down from high-level models to detailed design.

We'll reinforce these principles, in one way or another, in each subsequent chapter. We suggest that if you adopt them at the beginning of a software development project and stick with them, you will significantly increase your chances of success.

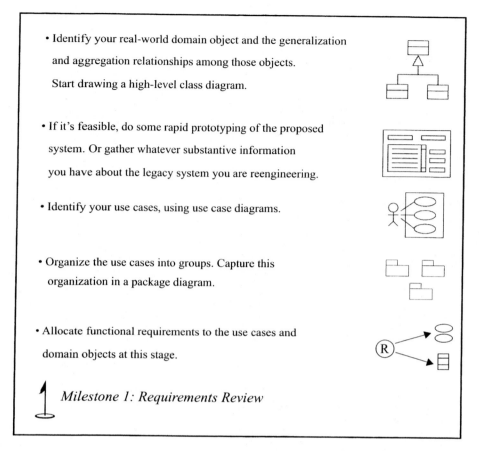

- Identify your real-world domain object and the generalization and aggregation relationships among those objects. Start drawing a high-level class diagram.

- If it's feasible, do some rapid prototyping of the proposed system. Or gather whatever substantive information you have about the legacy system you are reengineering.

- Identify your use cases, using use case diagrams.

- Organize the use cases into groups. Capture this organization in a package diagram.

- Allocate functional requirements to the use cases and domain objects at this stage.

Milestone 1: Requirements Review

Figure 1-8: *Requirements Analysis*

• Write descriptions of the use cases—basic courses of action
  that represent the "mainstream" and alternative courses
  for less-frequently traveled paths and error conditions.

• Perform robustness analysis. For each use case:

  – Identify a first cut of objects that accomplish the
    stated scenario. Use the UML Objectory
    stereotypes.

  – Update your domain-model class diagram with
    new objects and attributes as you discover them.

• Finish updating the class diagram so that it reflects
  the completion of the analysis phase of the project.

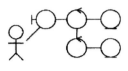

Milestone 2: Preliminary Design Review (PDR)

Figure 1-9: *Analysis and Preliminary Design*

• Allocate behavior. For each use case:

  – Identify the messages that need to be passed between objects,
    the objects, and the associated methods to be invoked.
    Draw a sequence diagram with use case text running
    down the left side and design information on the right.
    Continue to update the class diagram with attributes
    and operations as you find them.

  – If you wish, show, on a collaboration diagram,
    the key transactions between objects.

  – If you wish, use a state diagram to show the real-time behavior.

• Finish the static model by adding detailed design
  information (for instance, visibility values and patterns).

• Verify with your team that your design satisfies
  all the requirements you've identified.

Milestone 3: Critical Design Review (CDR)

Figure 1-10: *Design*

• As needed, produce diagrams, such as deployment and component
  diagrams, that will help you with the implementation phase.

• Write/generate the code.

• Perform unit and integration testing.

• Perform system and user-acceptance testing, using the use cases
  as black-box test cases for the latter.

Milestone 4: Delivery

Figure 1-11: *Implementation*

Requirements List for The Internet Bookstore

Starting in the next chapter, we're going to be following a running example, which we call The Internet Bookstore, through each phase of the process we've just outlined for you. The use cases we'll be working through, and the classes we'll discover, exist to satisfy certain requirements that our client (the owner of the bookstore we're going to build) has specified. These requirements include the following:

- The bookstore shall accept orders over the Internet.
- The bookstore shall maintain a list of accounts for up to 1,000,000 customers.
- The bookstore shall provide password protection for all accounts.
- The bookstore shall provide the ability to search the master book catalog.
- The bookstore shall provide a number of search methods on that catalog, including search by author, search by title, search by ISBN number, and search by keyword.
- The bookstore shall provide a secure means of allowing customers to pay by credit card.
- The bookstore shall provide a secure means of allowing customers to pay via purchase order.
- The bookstore shall provide a special kind of account that is preauthorized to pay via purchase order.
- The bookstore shall provide electronic links between the Web and database and the shipping fulfillment system.
- The bookstore shall provide electronic links between the Web and database and the inventory management system.
- The bookstore shall maintain reviews of books, and allow anyone to upload review comments.
- The bookstore shall maintain ratings on books, based on customer inputs.

Chapter 2

Domain Modeling

Domain modeling forms the foundation of the static part of our UML model. When we build a domain model, we start off by trying to identify abstractions in the real world—that is, the main conceptual objects that are going to participate in this system. When you design object-oriented software, you try to structure your software around these real-world, problem space objects. The theory behind this is that the real world changes less frequently than the software requirements. The basis for our whole object modeling activity, particularly the static modeling part of the activity, is a model of these problem domain abstractions.

You may be wondering why this chapter precedes a discussion of use cases in a book called *Applying Use Case Driven Object Modeling*. The reason is that when we write our use cases (see Chapter 3), we're not going to write them from an abstract, pure user viewpoint; instead, we're going to be writing *use cases in the context of the object model*. By doing this, we'll be able to link together the static and dynamic portions of the model, which is essential if we're going to drive the design forward from the use cases. The domain model serves as a *glossary of terms* that writers of use cases can use in the early stages of that effort.

As we identify real-world, problem domain objects, we also need to identify the relationships among those objects. These include two particularly important relationship types: **generalization**, which is the superclass/subclass relationship, and **aggregation**, which is the whole part/subpart kind of relationship. There are other types of relationships between classes in addition to generalization and aggregation, including plain vanilla associations between objects, but generalization and aggregation are particularly important. As the foundation of our static model, we're using UML class diagrams to express our domain model.

UML classes give us a place to capture **attributes**, which are data elements or data members, as well as **operations**, which are the functions that a given object performs. However, in the initial domain modeling activity, we don't usually want to spend too much time capturing attributes and operations—we'll do this later on as we refine and flesh out the static part of our model. We want to focus on identifying objects and the relationships between them as we're doing the domain modeling.

Reuse is one of the main goals of building your software around these real-world abstractions, because we often have multiple software systems that share a common problem domain. Keep in mind that if you're aiming for reuse, you want to do a very good job at domain modeling because the reusable aspects of your software are largely going to come out of this domain modeling activity. This domain model then becomes the foundation for the static part of your model.

The domain modeling process, for which we're following the Object Modeling Technique (OMT) school of thought, is fundamentally an inside-out approach. Inside-out means that we're starting with the core objects in the system, then working from the inside outward, to see how those objects are going to participate in the system we're building. So, the use case approach, or the dynamic part of the model, is an outside-in approach, whereas the static part of the model is an inside-out approach. The trick when you're working both outside-in and inside-out is to make these two parts meet in the middle and not have a disconnect in between. As we get into robustness analysis (see Chapter 5) and sequence diagrams (see Chapter 7), we'll see exactly how this works. For now, just keep in mind that this domain model and static modeling activity is really an inside-out look at our system.

Figure 2-1 shows where domain modeling resides within the "big picture" for the ICONIX process.

The Key Elements of Domain Modeling

The first thing you need to do in building a static model of your system is to find appropriate classes that accurately represent the real abstractions that the problem domain presents. If you execute this activity well, you will have not only a solid foundation on which to build the system but also excellent prospects for reuse by systems that will be designed and built down the line.

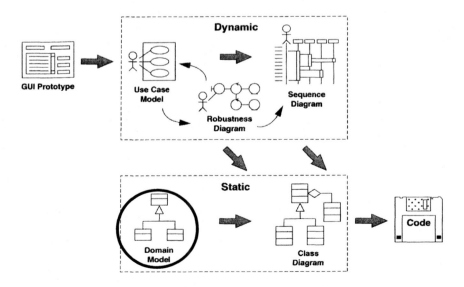

Figure 2-1: *Domain Modeling and the ICONIX Process*

The best sources of domain classes are likely to be the high-level problem statement, lower-level requirements, and expert knowledge of the problem space. To get started on the road to discovery, lay out as many relevant statements from these sources (and others, such as marketing literature) as you can find, and then circle or highlight all the nouns and noun phrases. Chances are that you will find a large majority of the important domain objects (classes) this way.

After refining the lists as work progresses, this is what tends to happen:

- Nouns and noun phrases become objects and attributes.
- Verbs and verb phrases become operations and associations.
- Possessive phrases indicate that nouns should be attributes rather than objects.

The next step is to sift through your list of candidate classes and eliminate the items that are unnecessary (because they're redundant or irrelevant) or incorrect (because they're too vague, they represent things or concepts outside the scope of the model, or they represent actions even though they're phrased as nouns).

While you're building your class diagram(s), you can also make some initial decisions about generalization ("kind of" or "is a" relationships among classes). If you need to, and if you're comfortable doing so at this stage of your project, you can generalize to more than one level of subclass. Remember to look for "kind of" statements that are true in the real world. Domain modeling is also the appropriate area for decisions about aggregations ("part of" or "has" relationships) among classes.

Finally, much like an entity-relationship diagram (ERD), our domain model, updated to show associations—the static relationships between pairs of classes—should be a true statement about the problem space, independent of time (that is, static). This model serves as the foundation of our static class model.

We recommend that you establish a time budget for building your initial domain model. You're not going to make it perfect, anyway, so do it quickly and expect to fix it up as you proceed. You should be vigilant about making necessary adjustments to your analysis-level class model in response to occurrences during robustness analysis and throughout the project.

The Top 10 Domain Modeling Errors

The flip side of the principles we just discussed takes the form of a number of common errors that our students make when they're doing domain modeling for their projects. Our "Top 10" list follows.

Start assigning multiplicities to associations right off the bat. Make sure that every association has an explicit multiplicity.

Some associations on a class diagram represent one-to-one relationships, whereas others represent one-to-many relationships. These are both called **multiplicities**. However, you should avoid dealing with multiplicity altogether during domain modeling—it chews up time and can be a major cause of analysis paralysis.

Do noun and verb analysis so exhaustive that you pass out along the way.

Kurt Derr's *Applying OMT* (SIGS Books, 1995) is a good source of information about "grammatical inspection." If you follow Derr's advice all the way down the line, though, you're likely to find yourself at too a low level of abstraction, in addition to running the risk of a nervous breakdown. Use the technique to get your object discovery started, but take care not to get carried away.

Assign operations to classes without exploring use cases and sequence diagrams.

We advocate a minimalist approach to defining operations during domain modeling. In fact, we're going to tell you that you shouldn't assign any operations to classes during domain modeling. That's because there isn't enough information available with which to make good design decisions about operations at that stage of a project. When we get to interaction modeling, however, we do have good information (at least we hope to). We describe interaction modeling in Chapter 7.

Optimize your code for reusability before making sure you've satisfied the user's requirements.

The more general your objects and classes, the higher the probability that you'll be able to reuse those objects and classes for other projects. And a complete class is one that is theoretically reusable in any number of contexts. However, to achieve reusability and completeness, you need to consider both attributes and operations, and we just told you why you shouldn't be assigning operations to classes during domain modeling, so it's not wise to overdo your efforts to make classes reusable when you're doing high-level class diagrams. Move quickly through domain modeling, so you have time to make sure that you're building what your customers want.

Debate whether to use aggregation or composition for each of your "part-of" associations.

Grady Booch's original descriptions of "has by reference" relationships morphed into aggregation within the UML. Similarly, "has by value" became a "strong" form of aggregation called **composition** within which a "piece" class is "owned by" a parent class: if the parent is deleted, all instances of the child get deleted automatically. Trying to differentiate between these two during a domain modeling effort is a surefire way to do some serious tail-chasing. We prefer to use simple aggregation during domain modeling. Aggregation versus composition is a detailed design issue.

Presume a specific implementation strategy without modeling the problem space.

As part of ongoing refinement of your domain model, you should remove anything that clearly states an action rather than a dependency or that's specifically related to implementation. What you should *not* do is start introducing things on your high-level class diagrams that represent commitments to specific technologies, such as a relational database or a particular kind of server. Leave implementation issues to implementation; model the problem domain first.

Use hard-to-understand names for your classes, like cPortMgrIntf, instead of intuitively obvious ones, like PortfolioManager.

One good reason to do domain modeling up front is to facilitate the task of getting everyone on the project team to agree on what your key abstractions should be called. The more obvious the class names, the easier that task will be. Save acronyms and other kinds of abbreviations (if you insist on having them) for implementation.

Jump directly to implementation constructs, such as friend relationships and parameterized classes.

The UML offers a lot of opportunities to add what we call "Booch stuff" to class diagrams. This includes constructs that came across more or less directly from C++, such as parameterized classes and friend relationships. These are much more relevant to the solution space than to the problem space, though, and the focus of domain modeling should definitely be the problem space.

Create a one-for-one mapping between domain classes and relational database tables.

If you're reengineering a legacy system that uses a relational database, the tables within that database are likely to be an excellent source of names for your domain classes. However, be careful not to just bring them over to your static model wholesale. A relational table can have a lot of attributes that might not belong together in the context of an object model. You should try to use aggregation to factor groups of attributes into "helper" classes, which contain attributes and operations that can be grouped into smaller "piece-part" classes.

Perform "premature patternization," which involves building cool solutions, from patterns, that have little or no connection to user problems.

Patterns often start becoming visible during robustness analysis. As we'll explore in Chapter 5, there are two strategies, "control in the screen" and "use case controller," that lend themselves to discovering patterns connected to use cases. Looking ahead, design patterns can be highly useful in the context of sequence diagrams and design-level class diagrams. Domain modeling is *not* the time to start thinking in terms of patterns.

Exercises

The following exercises, taken from the domain model for our Internet Bookstore, are designed to test your ability to spot the top 10 mistakes that people make during domain modeling. (The full domain model is presented at the end of the chapter and also in Appendix A.) Each page with a red label at the top contains three or four of these mistakes; your task is to write corrections on the page near the erroneous material. Following each of these pages is a page with a white label inside a black box at the top; this page contains corrected material and explanations of the top 10 rules that were violated on the previous page. Happy hunting!

Exercise 1

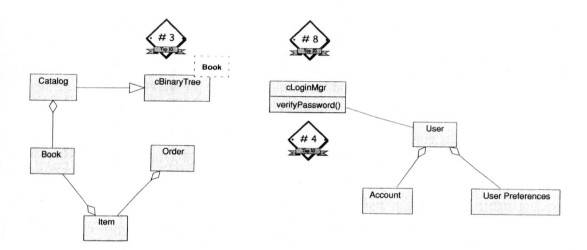

Exercise 1

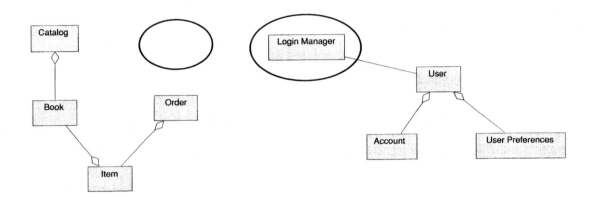

On the previous diagram:

- The cBinaryTree class is a parameterized class (also known as a template class within the UML). There's no good reason to start defining an implementation construct such as a binary tree at this stage of modeling.

- The cLoginMgr class has an operation named verifyPassword. It's too early to make decisions about which operations go on which classes, and besides, chances are good that the operation belongs on the Account class anyway.

- The name of the class we just discussed was not intuitively obvious.

Exercise 2

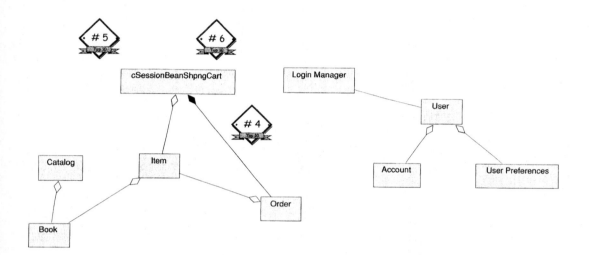

Exercise 2

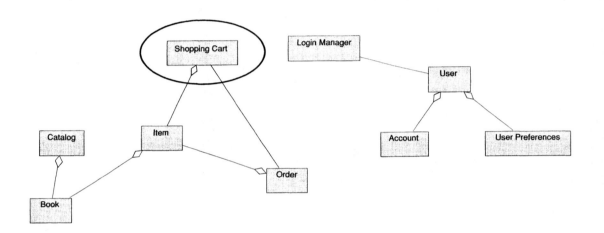

On the previous diagram:

- The name of the cSessionBeanShpngCart class indicated that the modeler decided to represent the concept of a shopping cart using a session Enterprise Java Bean (EJB). Robustness analysis, which we'll discuss in Chapter 5, is the appropriate stage to start exploring how to map classes to things such as beans.

- A class that represents a shopping cart should be called Shopping Cart.

- The class we've been discussing had a composition relationship with the Order class. The modeler committed to the idea that an Order disappears when the shopping cart object to which it belongs is destroyed. This may or not make sense in the long run, but it's certainly too soon to be thinking along those lines.

Exercise 3

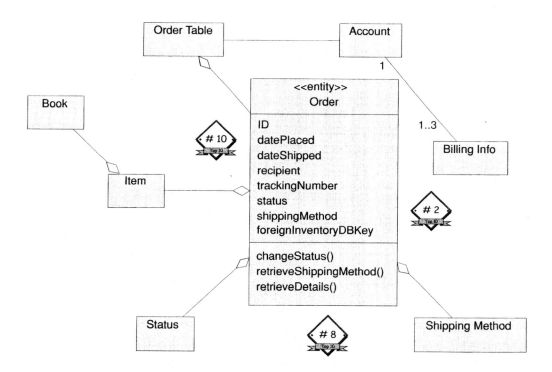

Exercise 3

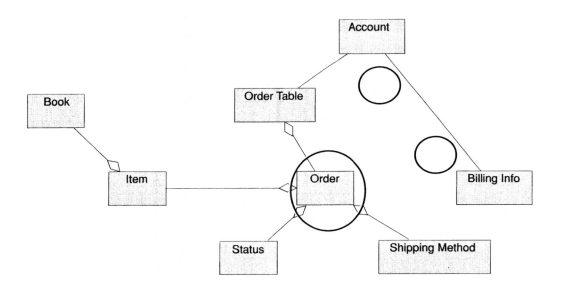

On the previous diagram:

- The presence of the foreignInventoryDBKey attribute indicates that the modeler is looking ahead toward a relational database. (Note also that classes in your domain model shouldn't have attributes yet, and they certainly shouldn't have operations.)
- The Order class has operations assigned to it.
- The association between Account and Billing Info has a multiplicity.

Exercise 4

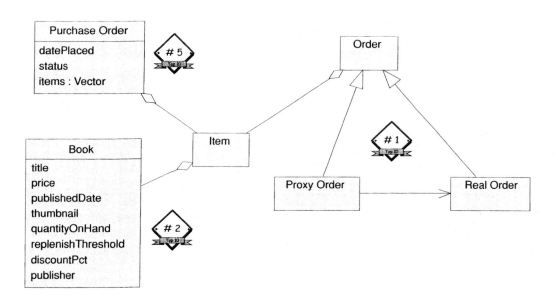

Exercise 4

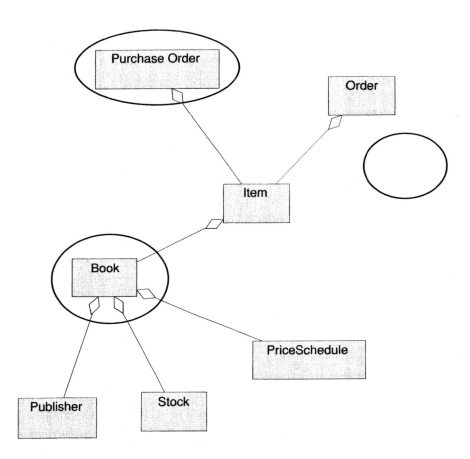

On the previous diagram:

- The presence of attributes named "price," "quantityOnHand," and "publisher," all of which probably belong in associated classes, indicates that the modeler is likely to have mapped an existing Order table directly to the Order class. (Also, as we mentioned for Exercise 3, classes in your domain model shouldn't have attributes yet.)

- The Purchase Order class uses the Vector construct from Java.

- The modeler has chosen to use the Proxy design pattern; domain modeling is too early to be making this decision.

Exercise 5

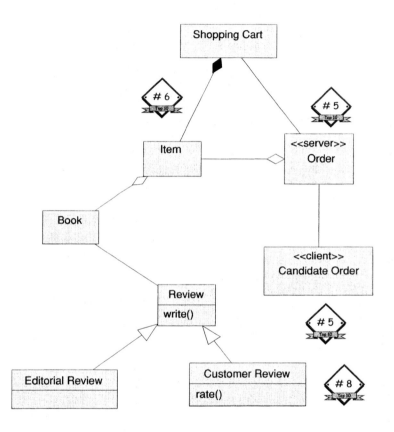

Exercise 5

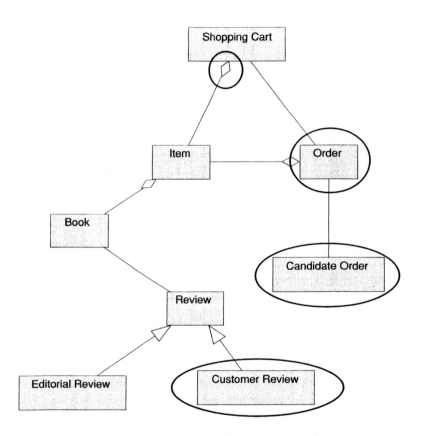

On the previous diagram:

- The Customer Review class has an operation.
- The association between Item and Shopping Cart is a composition, but it's too early to know whether this makes sense as opposed to an ordinary aggregation.
- The stereotypes on the Order and Candidate Order classes indicate a premature decision as to the layers to which the classes belong.

Bringing the Pieces Together

Figure 2-2 shows the full domain model for our Internet Bookstore. This diagram consolidates the fragments presented within the exercises and adds classes and associations that come into play later in this workbook.

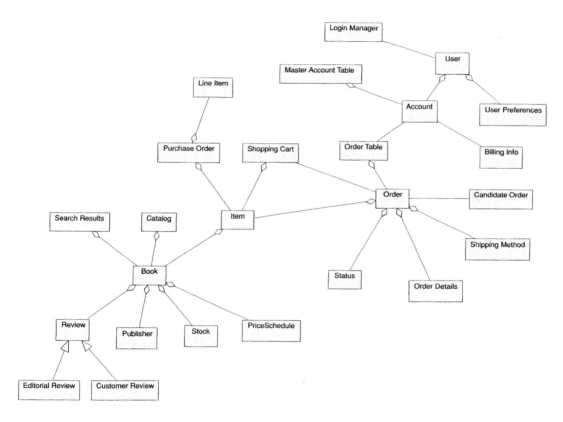

Figure 2-2: *Domain Model for The Internet Bookstore*

Chapter 3

Use Case Modeling

This chapter addresses a fundamental question that every development effort must ask: What are the users of the system trying to do? We're going to focus our efforts on trying to capture our users' actions, and the associated system responses, in great detail because the software behavior is dictated by the user requirements. In other words, what we need the software to do depends on how the users are accessing it and what the users are trying to do. This often relates to screens and user interfaces.

Figure 3-1 shows where use case modeling resides within the "big picture" for the ICONIX process. As you can see, we think it's a good idea to use prototypes to help define the use cases. And, we do our use case model, along with our domain model, right at the very beginning of our project. The entire dynamic part of the object model is directly driven from the use case model we put together. Since the dynamic model drives the static model, the use cases are also driving our static model, as well.

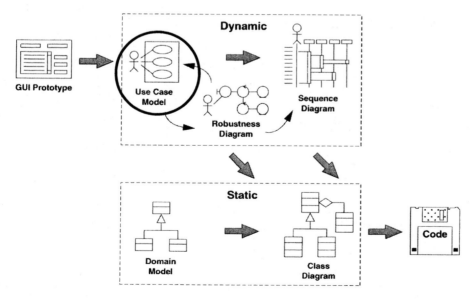

Figure 3-1: *The ICONIX Process Is Use Case Driven*

Figure 3-1 also shows that we're continuously updating and refining our static model based on further analysis of these use cases as we do our robustness and sequence diagrams. We're constantly updating our static model as we walk through the scenarios. That's how it evolves from the first-cut domain model to our detailed design-level static model. We're completely use case driven in this approach, in that our software architecture and our software design are both driven from our analysis of usage scenarios.

The whole dynamic model is very much an outside-in type of approach. We start with users who are outside our system, and we work our way in to expose all details of the software behavior. From that, the software structure that supports that behavior is created. But we're working inward from the outside of the system, one scenario at a time. Because the use cases are the fundamental unit of decomposition in this modeling effort, everything else is directly driven from this outside-in approach. As a result, we're reliably able to design systems that meet our user requirements, which is no small accomplishment.

The Key Elements of Use Case Modeling

The task of building use cases for your new system is based on identifying as many as you can up front and then establishing a continuous loop of writing and refining the text that describes them. Along the way, you will discover new use cases and also factor out commonality in usage.

You should keep one overriding principle in mind at all times in your effort to identify use cases: *They should have strong correlations with material in the user manual for the system.* It should be obvious what the connection is between each use case and a distinct section of your user guide. This reinforces the fundamental notion that you are conforming the design of your system to the viewpoints of the users. It also provides a convenient summary of what "use case driven" means: *Write the user manual, then write the code.* If you're reengineering a legacy system, you can simply work from the user manual backward, making any necessary changes as you go.

Once you have some text in place for a use case, it's time to refine it by making sure the sentences are clear and discrete, the basic format of your text is *noun-verb-noun*, and the actors and potential domain objects are easily identifiable. You should also update your domain model (see Chapter 2) as you discover new objects and expand your understanding of the objects you'd previously found. And, it's very important to think of all possible alternate courses of action for each use case wherever possible, which should be a large majority of the time. Note that robustness analysis (see Chapter 5) will be very helpful toward accomplishing all of this refinement.

Although some authors encourage the use of voluminous use case templates, here's what we recommend to *every one* of our clients:

1. *Create a use case template* that has areas labeled Basic Course and Alternative Courses. Don't put anything else in there; it'll just distract you.

2. *Ask "What happens?"* This will get the basic course of action started.

3. *Ask "And then what happens?"* Keep asking that question until you have all the details of your basic course on paper.

4. *Ask, "What else can happen?"* Be relentless. Are there *any* other things that can happen? Are you *sure*? Keep asking *those* questions until you have a rich set of alternative courses written down. Trust us: Grief at this point is much easier to take than grief during, say, integration testing.

The goal is *not* to construct an elegant use case model; the goal is to account for *everything* the user might do.

You'll review this material during a requirements review (see Chapter 4); you'll review it *again* during a preliminary design review (see Chapter 6); and you'll review it *once more* during a critical design review (see Chapter 8). This may seem excessive, but keep in mind that the more well-defined the system behavior, the easier it's going to be to build the system.

You can use several mechanisms to factor out common usage, such as error handling, from sets of use cases. This is usually a good thing to do because breaking usage down to atomic levels will make your analysis effort easier and save you a lot of time when you're drawing sequence diagrams. Whether you use the UML's use case generalization and *include* and *extend* relationships, or the *invoke* and *precede* relationships from the Open Modeling Language (OML), which we recommend in *Use Case Driven Object Modeling with UML*, your goal should be a set of small, precise, reusable use cases.

We recommend grouping use cases into packages, primarily because these packages form logical boundaries for dividing work among subteams. A good rule to follow is: *Each package should correspond with a chapter, or at least a major section, in your user manual.*

You should feel comfortable proceeding to the next phases of the development process when you've achieved the following goals of use case modeling:

- You've built use cases that together account for *all* of the desired functionality of the system.

- You've produced clear and concise written descriptions of the basic course of action, along with appropriate alternative courses of action, for each use case.

- You've factored out scenarios common to more than one use case, using whichever constructs you're most comfortable using.

The Top 10 Use Case Modeling Errors

The flip side of the principles we just discussed takes the form of a number of common errors that we have seen students make when they're doing use case modeling on their projects for the first time. Our "Top 10" list follows.

Write functional requirements instead of usage scenario text.

Requirements are generally stated in terms of what the system shall do. Usage scenarios describe actions that the users are taking and the responses that the system generates. Eventually, we're going to use our use case text as a runtime behavioral spec for the scenario we're describing, and this text will sit on the left margin of a sequence diagram. We want to be able to easily see *how* the system (shown with objects and messages) is implementing the *desired behavior*, as described in the use case text. So, we need to keep a clear distinction between (active voice) usage descriptions (behavior) and (passive voice) system requirements.

Describe attributes and methods rather than usage.

Not only shouldn't your use case text include too many presentation details, but it should be relatively free of details about the fields on your screens, as well. Field names often match up directly with the names of attributes on your domain classes, which we talked about in Chapter 2. If you find yourself starting to list the names of, say, 13 fields from the screen in your use case text, stop. Open the domain model, find the class(es) where those attributes belong, and capture them where they'll do you some good—as attributes. Later, when you need them, they'll be there. Methods shouldn't be named or described in case text because they represent *how* the system will do things, as opposed to *what* the system will do.

Write the use cases too tersely.

When it comes to writing text for use cases, expansive is preferable to terse. You're going to need to address all of the details of user actions and system responses as you move into robustness analysis and interaction modeling, so you might as well put some of those details in your use cases up front. Remember also that your use cases will serve as the foundation for your user manual, and it's always better to err on the side of too much detail rather than not enough when it comes to user documentation.

Divorce yourself completely from the user interface.

One of the fundamental notions of "use case driven" is that the development team conforms the design of the system to the viewpoints of the users. You can't do this without being specific as to what actions the users will be performing on your screens. As we mentioned for item 9, you don't need to talk about fields in your use case text, and you also don't want to go into any detail about the cosmetic appearance of your screens; you can let your prototypes, in whatever form they take, do that work for you. You *do*, however, need to discuss those features of the user interface that allow the user to *tell the system to do something*.

Avoid explicit names for your boundary objects.

Boundary objects are the objects with which actors will be interacting. These frequently include windows, screens, dialogs, and menus. In keeping with our themes of including ample detail and being explicit about user navigation, we submit that it's necessary to name your boundary objects explicitly in your use case text. Another reason that it's important to do this is that you're going to explore the behavior of these objects during robustness analysis (see Chapter 5), and it can only help reduce ambiguity and confusion to name them early.

Write using a perspective other than the user's, in passive voice.

A use case is most effectively stated from the perspective of the user as a set of *present-tense verb phrases in active voice.* The tendency of engineers to use passive voice is well-established, but use cases should state the actions that the user performs, and the system's responses to those actions, and this kind of text is only effective when it's stated in active voice.

Describe only user interactions; ignore system responses.

The narrative of a use case should be event-response oriented, as in, "The system does this when the user does that." The use case should capture a good deal of what happens "under the covers" in response to what the actor is doing, such as creating new objects, validating user input, or generating error messages. Remember that your use case text describes both sides of the dialog between the user and the system, and that *all of the software behavior that you're trying to discover happens on the system side of that dialog.* If you leave out the system responses, you ignore the software behavior.

Omit text for alternative courses of action.

Basic courses of action are generally easier to identify and write text for. That doesn't mean, however, that you should put off dealing with alternative courses until, say, detailed design. In fact, it's been our experience that when important alternative courses of action are not uncovered until coding and debugging, the programmer responsible for writing or fixing the code tends to treat them in ways that are most convenient for him or her. Needless to say, this isn't healthy for a project.

Focus on something other than what's "inside" a use case, such as how you get there or what happens afterward.

Several prominent authors advocate the use of long, complicated use case templates. Spaces for preconditions and postconditions are generally present on these templates. We like to think of this as the 1040 "long form" approach to use case modeling, in comparison to the 1040EZ-like template that we advocate (two headings: *Basic Course* and *Alternate Course*). You shouldn't insist on using long and complex use case templates just because they appeared in a book or article. Don't waste your time.

Spend a month deciding whether to use includes *or* extends.

In our years of teaching use case driven development, we have yet to come across a situation in which we've needed more than one mechanism for factoring out commonality. Whether you use the UML's *include* construct, or the OML's *invoke* and *precede* mechanisms, or something else that you're comfortable with, doesn't matter; what matters is that you pick one way of doing things and stick with it. Having two similar constructs is worse than having only one. It's too easy to get confused—and bogged down—when you try to use both. Don't spin your wheels.

Exercises

The following exercises, taken from the use case model for our Internet Bookstore, are designed to test your ability to spot the top 10 mistakes that people make during use case modeling. (The full use case model is presented in Appendix A.) Each page with a red label at the top contains three or four of these mistakes; your task is to write corrections on the page near the erroneous material. Following each of these pages is a page with a white label inside a black box at the top; this page contains corrected material (in italics) and explanations of the top 10 rules that were violated on the previous page. Happy hunting!

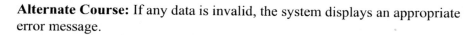

Exercise 1

[from Open Account]

Basic Course: The Customer enters the required information. The system validates the information and creates a new Account object.

Alternate Course: If any data is invalid, the system displays an appropriate error message.

[from Search by Author]

The user submits the request. The system displays another page that contains the search results.

[from Log In]

The Customer enters his or her user ID and password, and then clicks the Log In button. The system returns the Customer to the Home Page.

Exercise 1

Basic Course: *The Customer types his or her name, an email address, and a password (twice), and then presses the Create Account button.* The system ensures that the Customer has provided valid data, and then *creates an Account* object using that data. *Then the system returns the Customer to the Home Page.*

Alternate Courses:

- *If the Customer did not provide a name, the system displays an error message to that effect and prompts the Customer to type a name.*

- *If the Customer provided an email address that's not in the correct form, the system displays an error message to that effect and prompts the Customer to type a different address.*

- *If the Customer provided a password that is too short, the system displays an error message to that effect and prompts the Customer to type a longer password.*

- *If the Customer did not type the same password twice, the system displays an error message to that effect and prompts the Customer to type the password correctly the second time.*

The Customer types the name of an Author on the Search Page, and then presses the Search button. The system...retrieves all of the Books with which that Author is associated....Then the system displays the list of Books on the Search Results Page.

Basic Course: The Customer enters his or her user ID and password, and then clicks the Log In button. *The system validates the login information against the persistent Account data, and then* returns the Customer to the Home Page.

Alternate Course: If the system cannot find the specified userID,

On the previous page:

- The first use case is too terse. There's no reference to what kind of information the Customer is entering, nor to the page he or she is looking at. The text doesn't explain what's involved in the validation of the data the Customer entered. And the use case doesn't describe how the Customer needs to respond to an error condition.

- The second use case fragment doesn't contain explicit names for the relevant boundary objects.

- The third use case fragment is lacking alternate courses, even though it should be fairly obvious from the context that some validation needs to occur and that there are several possible error conditions.

Exercise 2

[from Log In]

Name: Log In

Goal: To log a customer into the system.

Precondition: The Customer is not already logged into the system.

Basic Course: The Customer enters his or her user ID and password, and then clicks the Log In button....

Alternate Courses: ...

Postcondition: The Customer is logged into the system.

[from Edit Contents of Shopping Cart]

On the Shopping Cart Page, the Customer modifies the quantity of an Item in the Shopping Cart, and then presses the Update button. Then the Customer presses the Continue Shopping button.

[from Cancel Order]

Basic Course: The system displays the relevant information for the Order on the Cancel Order Page, including its contents and the shipping address. The Customer presses the Confirm Cancel button...

Exercise 2

Basic Course: The Customer enters his or her user ID and password, and then clicks the Log In button....

On the Shopping Cart Page, the Customer modifies the quantity of an Item in the Shopping Cart, and then presses the Update button. *The system stores the new quantity, and then computes and displays the new cost for that Item....*

Basic Course: *The system ensures that the Order is cancellable (in other words, that its status isn't "shipping" or "shipped").* Then the system displays the relevant information for the Order on the Cancel Order Page, including its contents and the shipping address. The Customer presses the Confirm Cancel button. *The system marks the Order status as "deleted," and then invokes the Return Items to Inventory use case.*

Alternate Course: *If the status of the Order is "shipping" or "shipped," the system displays a message indicating that it's too late for the Customer to cancel the order.*

On the previous page:

- The first use case fragment shows how useless it can be to be obsessive about using a complicated use case template. The name of the use case expresses the goal clearly enough; the content of the basic course will make the stated precondition and postcondition quite redundant.
- The second use case fragment doesn't specify what the system does in response to the Customer pressing the Update button, including possibly deleting an Item.
- The third use case fragment doesn't allow for the possibility that the Order might have a status that prevents it from being cancelled.

Exercise 3

[from Search by Author]

The Customer types the name of an Author, and then submits a search request….The system retrieves the important details about each Book, and then displays the list of Books.

[from Edit Contents of Shopping Cart]

Basic Course: If the Customer modifies the quantity of an Item in the Shopping Cart, and then presses the Update button, the system will store the new quantity, and then compute and display the new cost for that Item….

Alternate Course: The system will delete an Item from the Shopping Cart if the quantity of that Item in that Shopping Cart becomes 0.

[from Process Received Shipment]

The Receiving Clerk ensures that the Line Items listed on the Purchase Order match the physical items. The Clerk waves the bar code on the packing slip under the sensor at the receiving station. The system executes a "change order status" method to change the Order status to "fulfilled,"and then calls the changeQuantityOnHand method for each of the variousBooks. The Clerk hands the Books off to the Inventory Clerk.

Exercise 3

The Customer types the name of an Author *on the Search Page,* and then presses the Search button.... The system retrieves the important details about each Book....Then the system displays the list of *Books on the Search Results Page....*

Basic Course: On the Shopping Cart Page, *the Customer modifies* the quantity of an Item in the Shopping Cart, and then presses the Update button. The system *stores* the new quantity, and then *computes and displays* the new cost for that Item....

Alternate Course: *If the Customer changes the quantity of the Item to 0,* the system *deletes* that Item from the Shopping Cart.

The Receiving Clerk ensures that the Line Items listed on the Purchase Order match the physical items. The Clerk waves the bar code on the packing slip under the sensor at the receiving station. *The system changes the status of the Purchase Order to "fulfilled" and updates the quantity on hand values for the various Books.* The Clerk hands the Books off to the Inventory Clerk.

On the previous page:

- The first use case fragment doesn't name the boundary object.
- The second use case fragment reads more like part of a requirements spec than a use case.
- The third use case fragment refers to two methods.

Exercise 4

[from Check Out]

The Customer selects a billing method and presses the Use This Billing Information button. Then the Customer presses the Confirm Order button. The use case ends.

[from Ship Order]

The Clerk waves the bar code on the packing slip under the sensor at the shipping station. The system changes the status of the Order to "shipping." Then the system retrieves the Shipping Method that the Customer specified for this Order, and displays it on the Shipping Station Console....

[from Track Recent Orders]

The Customer clicks on a link. The system retrieves and displays the Contents of the Order, in view-only mode, on the Order Details Page. This display shows the relevant values of the Order object at the top of the page and the Item details, including the basics about each Book that the Customer ordered (but not the thumbnails), below that. The Customer presses OK to return to the Order Tracking Page.

Exercise 4

The Customer selects a billing method and presses the Use This Billing Information button. *The system associates the given Billing Info object with the Candidate Order. Then the system displays the Confirm Order Page.*

The Customer presses the Confirm Order button. *The system converts the Candidate Order to an Order and destroys the Shopping Cart. Then the system returns control to the use case from which this use case received control.*

Basic Course: *The Shipping Clerk ensures that the Items listed on the packing slip for the Order match the physical items.* The Clerk waves the bar code on the packing slip under the sensor at the shipping station. The system changes the status of the Order to "shipping." Then the system retrieves the Shipping Method that the Customer specified for this Order, and displays it on the Shipping Station Console....

Alternate Course: *If the Shipping Clerk finds a mismatch between the Order and the physical items, the Clerk stops processing of the Order until he or she is able to make a match.*

The Customer clicks on a link. The system retrieves and displays the contents of the Order, in view-only mode, on the Order Details Page. *[note missing text]* The Customer presses OK to return to the Order Tracking Page.

On the previous page:

- The first use case fragment doesn't describe what happens when the Customer presses the Use This Billing Information button or when he or she presses Confirm Order.
- The second use case fragment doesn't allow for the possibility that the set of Items that the Shipping Clerk has in front of him or her doesn't match what's on the packing slip.
- The third use case contains too many details about what the Order Details page will look like.

Exercise 5

[from Ship Order]

The Clerk finishes packaging the Order, and records the tracking number, and then sends the package out via the associated Shipper.

[from Track Recent Orders]

The system retrieves and displays the Orders that the Customer has Placed within the last 30 days....The Customer requests details for an Order. The system retrieves and displays the contents of the Order, in view-only mode. The Customer returns to the list of Orders when he or she is finished looking at the details of the given Order.

[from Browse List of Books]

The Customer clicks on a Category on the Browse Books Page. The System invokes the "displayYourSubcategories" method on the Category object. This process continues until there are no more subcategories, at which point the system displays the Books in the lowest subcategory.

Exercise 5

The Clerk weighs the set of physical items. The Clerk packages the Items. The Clerk attaches a manifest appropriate for the given shipping method. The Clerk waves the bar code on the manifest under the sensor. The system records the tracking number from the bar code for the given Order. The Clerk sends the package out via the associated Shipper.

The system retrieves the Orders that the Customer has placed within the last 30 days, *and displays these Orders on the Order Tracking Page. Each entry has the Order ID (in the form of a link), ...* The Customer clicks on a link. The system retrieves and displays the contents of the Order, in view-only mode, *on the Order Details Page. The Customer presses OK to return to the Order Tracking Page.*

The Customer clicks on a Category on the Browse Books Page. *The system displays the subcategories within that Category.* This process continues until there are no more subcategories, at which point the system displays the Books in the lowest subcategory.

On the previous page:

- The first use case fragment doesn't specify how the Shipping Clerk records the tracking number and thus how it gets associated with the given Order.
- The second use case fragment omits several details about where the list of Orders and the Order details appear and how the Customer navigates between these.
- The third use case fragment describes what happens in terms of a method rather than from the actor's standpoint.

Bringing the Pieces Together

Figure 3-2 shows the full use case diagram for our Internet Bookstore. This diagram shows the use cases that provide the fragments presented within the exercises, along with the actors involved in those use cases.

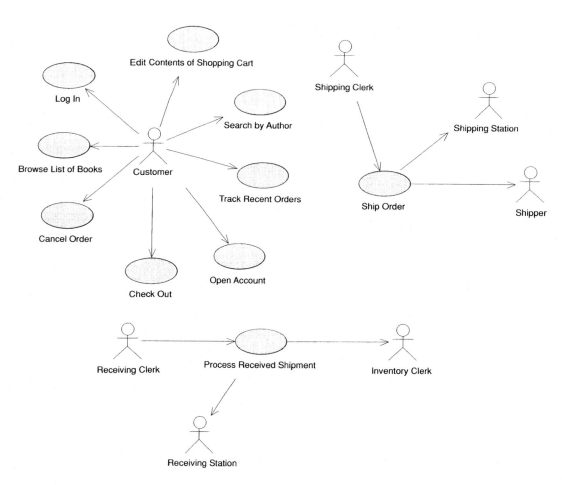

Figure 3-2: *Use Case Diagram for The Internet Bookstore*

Chapter 4

Requirements Review

Requirements review involves trying to ensure that the use cases and the domain model work together to address the customers' functional requirements. It also involves making sure that the customers have enough of an idea of what they want that our development team is able to base a design on those requirements. Some schools of thought hold that "customers never know what they want. . . the requirements change weekly, sometimes daily, even hourly," and use this to justify skipping analysis and design. This is an enormous cop-out. It's the analyst's job to help the customers focus their understanding of their requirements. Use cases, prototypes, and domain models are among the tools we can use to make this process work.

Figure 4-1 shows where we are.

The Key Elements of Requirements Review

Requirements review must involve representatives of both the customer(s) and the development team, as well as any necessary managers. The goal is to achieve basic agreement among all parties that the use cases, together with the domain model and whatever prototype elements are in place, capture the functional requirements of the system. This works best when everyone is in a room together, with a facilitator/moderator who keeps the conversations on track and a scribe who records the results and the action items. The key word is *traceability*: it should be clear how each requirement traces into one or more use cases, and how one or more classes from the domain model and one or more elements of the prototype work together with those use cases to address the requirement.

One of the fundamental questions that every development effort must ask is this: What are the real-world objects we need to model, and how do they relate to each other? Within the ICONIX process, domain modeling forms the foundation of the static part of our UML model. When we build a domain model, we start by trying to identify abstractions in the real world—that is, the main conceptual objects that are going to participate in this system.

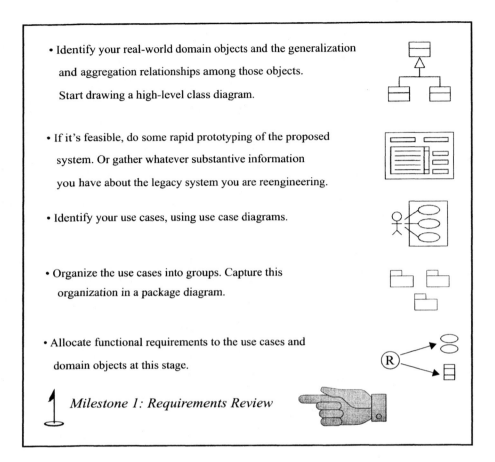

Figure 4-1: *Requirements Review and the ICONIX Process*

When you design object-oriented software, you try to structure your software around these real-world, problem space objects because the real world changes less frequently than the software requirements. The basis for our whole object modeling activity, particularly the static modeling part of the activity, is a model of these problem domain abstractions. You're going to evolve the initial class diagrams that show the domain model to the point where you can code from them, so it's critical that you capture the key abstractions early and effectively.

Another of those fundamental questions for a development effort is this: What are the users of the system trying to do? During use case modeling, and, by extension, requirements review, we're going to focus our efforts on trying to nail down our users' behavior in great detail, because the software behavior is dictated by the user requirements. In other words, what we need the software to do depends on how the users are accessing it and what the users are trying to do. Keep in mind that the more well-defined the system behavior, the easier it's going to be to build the system.

As you can see from Figure 1-1, we think it's a good idea to use prototypes to help define the use cases. We encourage our clients to use rapid prototyping as frequently as possible. The idea is that developers and users sit down together and build something that will demonstrate "proof of concept." However—and this is the big "however" that separates us from the eXtreme Programming (XP) community—*don't mistake your proof of concept prototype for deliverable, shippable software*—even if you've run some unit tests 300 or so times—unless you're fond of your users pressing **Ctrl-Alt-Delete** when confronted with the "blue screen of death."

Proof of concept prototypes are built with the goal of rapid delivery at the expense of robust, "bulletproof" design. When you're trying to demonstrate proof of concept, you're trying to get something that looks cosmetically close to what your users might be seeing built, as fast as you possibly can. So, you're likely to "do the simplest thing that can possibly work," to borrow a catchy slogan. It's like bringing in a construction crew to put up a movie set: They can build a "house" (actually a facade of a house) that looks fantastic from the outside, in just a small fraction of the time it takes to build a real house, but imagine trying to refactor this movie facade into a real house. For a real house, you need blueprints, electrical schematics, and plans for the plumbing. Always keep in mind that your proof of concept prototypes are just like movie set facade houses. What do you do if you have pointy-haired management that can't tell the difference? It's simple. Don't build your prototypes in code. Just work with pencil and paper line drawings. Some of our clients use an abstraction of the GUI called an **interaction flow diagram** very effectively for this purpose. This is essentially a large sheet of paper that shows small line drawings of the screens and the options for navigating among them.

Taking this idea one step further, we've found that exploring the graphical user interface (GUI) design in parallel with the required system behavior is generally an excellent approach. This involves iterating, with the users, the presentation aspects of the system, and after achieving closure on a couple of screens, writing the associated use cases. This bouncing back and forth can be very effective in the right environment. You should extend this thinking to your requirements review: the text for a given use case should match up well with the associated GUI element(s), in terms of the use case's descriptions of the basic nature of those elements and the system's responses to actions that the actor performs.

Some prominent people in the object-oriented (OO) community advocate the opposite: They insist that you shouldn't talk about GUI specifics in your use case text. They also insist that you shouldn't talk about much of anything specific, that you should leave your text as abstract (or **teleocentric**, which means goal-oriented) as possible. ("Teleocentric" is our favorite new vocabulary word.) We believe that you can't drive an abstract use case down through code nearly as effectively as you can drive a specific use case. You shouldn't talk about whether this field contains a set of radio buttons, or that window has both vertical and horizontal scroll bars in your use cases, but you should definitely talk about the "call and response," of actor and system, respectively, and you should name the objects that come into play, as well. Doing this is the best way to ensure a high level of traceability of your use cases into your analysis and design.

You should also do a grammar check on your use text during requirements review. A use case is most effectively stated from the perspective of the user as a set of *present-tense verb phrases in active voice*. The tendency of engineers to use passive voice is well-established (know anybody who writes like this: "The engineer shall use passive voice to articulate all possible behavioral options that may be presented by the system."?). However, as we just said, use cases should state the actions that the user performs and the system's responses to those actions, and this kind of text is only effective when it's stated in active voice.

Another critical aspect of use case modeling involves alternate courses of action. As we explained in Chapter 3, it's very important to think of all possible alternate courses of action for each use case wherever possible, which should be a large majority of the time, by asking, "What *else* can happen? Are there *any* other things that can happen? Are you *sure*?"

As we described in Chapter 3, you should also stay away from long, complicated use case templates that have spaces for the likes of preconditions and postconditions along with many other things that tend to be redundant at best and annoying at worst.

The Top 10 Requirements Review Errors

The flip side of the principles we just discussed takes the form of a number of common errors that our students make when they're doing requirements review for their projects. Our "Top 10" list follows.

Don't review requirements at all. Instead, invite "feature-itis" by letting the coders build whatever they want.

One of the fundamental tenets of XP is that since requirements change every day, it doesn't make much sense to try to deal with them explicitly. People who follow this approach, or something similar, lose not only traceability of requirements but also the ability to build trust between customers and developers that can only result from intensive face-to-face negotiation. The likely outcome is that coders build a cool system that doesn't have a whole lot to do with what the customers think they're paying for.

The XP folks even have cool slogans to describe this phenomenon. Kent Beck used it to diagnose the failure of the C3 project (XP's big claim to fame) on their Wiki Website: "...the fundamental problem was [that] the Gold Owner and Goal Donor weren't the same. The customer feeding stories to the team didn't care about the same things as the managers evaluating the team's performance....The new customers who came on wanted tweaks to the existing system more than they wanted to turn off the next mainframe payroll system. IT management wanted to turn off the next mainframe payroll system." Translating: In XP lingo, the Goal Donor is the customer representative who sits in the room with the coders, who explain that it's okay to change requirements in midstream, while the Gold Owner is the project sponsor—the one who owns the gold. In the case of C3 (which was a Y2K mainframe payroll replacement project), the Gold Owner "inexplicably" pulled the plug in February of 2000 when the program (no doubt complete with cool features) was only paying one third of the employees, after something on the order of four years of labor. (We suggest that you visit **http://c2.com/cgi/wiki?CthreeProjectTerminated** and think very carefully about what it says there.)

Would requirements reviews have saved this project? We can't say for certain. But we can say that "feature-itis," which comes at the expense of schedule, is a common and predictable result of letting the programming team decide (and continuously change) the priority of the requirements (in other words, make it up as they go along) and not reviewing this prioritization with the "gold owner" project sponsors.

Don't make sure the use case text matches the desired system behavior.

The phrase "use case driven" refers to the principle of using use cases, which capture the "what" that the system needs to do, to drive analysis, design, testing, and implementation (the "how"). If your use case text doesn't offer high correlations with what your users want the system to do, you're going to build the wrong system. Period.

Don't use any kind of GUI prototype or screen mockup to help validate system behavior.

Prototypes, whether they take the form of fully workable front ends, drawings on scraps of paper, or something in between, generally provide a "jump start" for the task of discovering and exploring use cases. Making sure that your use case text matches the navigation that a prototype shows is an excellent way to ensure that you're going to build the right system. If you don't have any visual frame of reference, you run the risk that user interface people will build stuff that doesn't match your users' requirements as expressed in the use cases.

Keep your use cases at such a high level of abstraction that your nontechnical clients have no clue what they're about.

Good use cases have enough details to enable their use in driving the development of a system from requirements discovery all the way through code. They also serve as a very effective tool for negotiating requirements with customers and managing customer expectations. This only works, though, if the use case text is specific: the actor does this, the system does this. A customer can't sign off on a use case that he or she doesn't understand.

Don't make sure that the domain model accurately reflects the real-world conceptual objects.

You're going to build code from class diagrams that have ample detail on them. These diagrams evolve from high-level class diagrams that show the initial domain model as you explore the dynamic behavior of the system you're designing. This evolution simply won't happen the way it should if you don't get the right set of domain objects in place to start with.

Don't make sure the use case text references the domain objects.

The main reason we discussed domain modeling (in Chapter 2) before we talked about use case modeling (in Chapter 3) is that a key goal of domain modeling is to build a glossary of terms for use case text to use. This technique will help you considerably in your effort to be specific in your use cases, and it'll also help you focus on traceability, because your use cases and your class diagrams will work together. Plus, it's quite a bit easier to do robustness analysis (the subject of Chapter 5) quickly if you've already named your objects in your use case text.

Don't question any use case with no alternate courses of action.

It's been our experience that upwards of 90 percent of good use cases have at least one alternate course of action. The appearance of a word such as "check" or "ensure" or "validate" or "verify" in use text is a clear signal that there's at least one alternate course, associated with an error condition. A use case is also likely to have at least one path that the actor takes more frequently than the one specified by the basic course. You need to be diligent about digging for these other paths.

Don't question whether all alternate courses of action have been considered on every use case.

One technique that works well in finding alternate courses is to question every sentence in your basic course. What could possibly go wrong? Is there something else that the actor could do besides this action? Could the system respond in different ways? As we stated earlier, you should be relentless in your search for alternate courses; much of the interesting behavior of your system will be reflected in them, *not* in the basic courses.

Don't worry if your use cases are written in passive voice.

Your use cases should describe actions: ones that the actors perform, and ones that the system performs. Actions are best expressed with action verbs, and active voice is the appropriate voice for action verbs. Passive voice is appropriate only when the writer doesn't know who or what is performing a given action, and that should never be the case within use case text.

Don't worry if your use cases are four pages long.

The basic course of a use case should be one or two paragraphs long. Each alternate course should be a sentence or two. Sometimes you'll have shorter use cases, especially when they serve as "connecting tissue" (for example, use cases centered around selecting from a menu). And there are times when you need longer use cases. But you should use techniques such as the *invokes* and *precedes* constructs we talk about in *Use Case Driven Object Modeling with UML* to factor out common behavior so that you can write concise use cases that you're more likely to be able to reuse—and you should definitely stay away from lengthy use case templates that generate considerably more heat than light.

Chapter 5

Robustness Analysis

There are two major questions that help us link the dynamic model with the static model. The first question is: What objects do we need for each of these use cases? (We'll pose the second question in Chapter 7.) We'll use the robustness analysis technique originally developed by Ivar Jacobson to help answer this question.

A **robustness diagram** is similar to a UML collaboration diagram, in that it shows the objects that participate in the scenario and how those objects interact with each other. Robustness analysis is not exactly a core part of UML; instead, it requires the use of some stereotypes. Robustness analysis was part of Jacobson's Objectory method; it's an informal, "back of the envelope" kind of analysis that's of enormous value in helping you refine use case text and discover objects that are needed, but that didn't make it into the domain model.

When they built the UML, the three amigos recognized the existence of this technique, but they didn't incorporate it as a core part of the UML standard. Instead, they developed Objectory process-specific extensions. They did this using a UML technique called **stereotyping**, which allows you to bind custom icons to any kind of symbol. In the case of robustness analysis, stereotypes implement the icons you see on the screen as icons for classes.

Anatomically, a robustness diagram in UML is a class diagram, although Jacobson's original concept was closer to a collaboration diagram, which shows object instances rather than classes. Today, though, it's a class diagram on which, instead of showing the normal UML class symbol, you use three kinds of icons, for three different kinds of objects:

1. **Boundary objects**, which actors use in communicating with the system
2. **Entity objects**, which are usually objects from the domain model (the subject of Chapter 2)
3. **Control objects** (which we usually call **controllers** because they often aren't real objects), which serve as the "glue" between boundary objects and entity objects

Figure 5-1 shows the visual icons for these three types of objects.

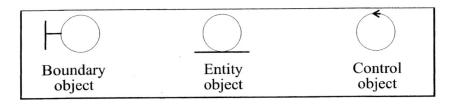

Figure 5-1: *Robustness Diagram Symbols*

Within the ICONIX process, this simple but highly useful technique serves as a crucial link between analysis (the *what)* and design (the *how)*, as shown in Figure 5-2.

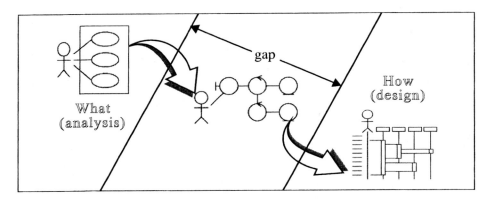

Figure 5-2: *Robustness Analysis Bridges the Gap Between What and How*

This diagram explains a lot about why software development, in general, is a hard process. What we're talking about is the need to start from a requirements-level view, where you're thinking only about *what* your users need to do with the system without considering implementation details, and then driving that view of your system forward into something that's totally focused on design. In this case, on your sequence diagram (see Chapter 7), you're showing precisely *how* runtime object instances interact with each other as your system is executing. One of the most difficult problems in software development is to get from this "what" view of the world into a "how" view of the world. Robustness analysis is a technique that helps people do this.

At this preliminary design phase, you should start to think through possible alternative design strategies and technical architectures that are going to differ, depending on what technologies you're using to build the system. You're going to start to uncover issues related to system performance. For example, you may find that you have two objects that need to have heavy communication with each other and that these objects are remotely connected across a network. This may have performance implications for your design. During robustness analysis, you'll take your requirements-level use case text and start making some preliminary design assumptions.

It's curious that most of the current body of UML literature doesn't make any mention of this concept. Our experience is that *success on your projects and avoiding analysis paralysis is directly linked to using this technique.*

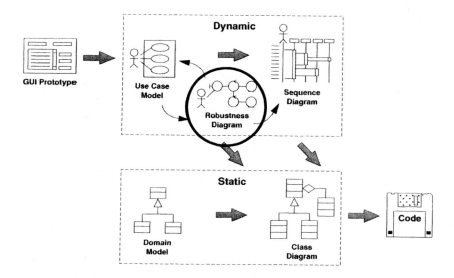

Figure 5-3: *Robustness Analysis Helps You Refine the Use Case Text and the Domain Model*

Figure 5-3 shows where robustness analysis resides within the "big picture" for the ICONIX process.

The Key Elements of Robustness Analysis

Robustness analysis plays several essential roles within the ICONIX process. Note that you will refine both your use case text and your static model as a result of robustness analysis, as shown in Figure 5-4.

- It provides a *sanity check* by helping you make sure that your use case text is correct and that you haven't specified system behavior that's unreasonable—or impossible—given the set of objects you have to work with. This refinement of the use case text changes the nature of that text from a pure user manual perspective to a usage description *in the context of the object model.*

- It also provides a *completeness and correctness check* by helping you make sure the use cases address all necessary alternate courses of action (which we discussed in Chapter 3). In our experience, the time spent drawing robustness diagrams toward this end, and also toward the end of producing text that adheres to some well-defined guidelines, *is invariably made up threefold or fourfold in time saved in drawing sequence diagrams*, which we'll talk about in Chapter 7.

- It enables *ongoing discovery of objects*, which is important because you almost certainly missed some objects during domain modeling. You can also address object naming discrepancies and conflicts before they cause serious problems. And, robustness analysis helps ensure that we've identified most of the entity and boundary classes *before* starting sequence diagrams.

- And, it serves the role of *preliminary design*, by closing the gap between analysis and detailed design, as we mentioned at the beginning of the chapter.

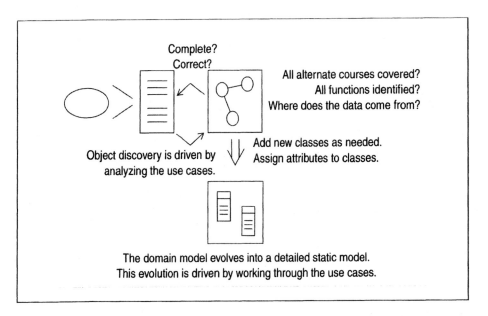

Complete?
Correct?

All alternate courses covered?
All functions identified?
Where does the data come from?

Object discovery is driven by
analyzing the use cases.

Add new classes as needed.
Assign attributes to classes.

The domain model evolves into a detailed static model.
This evolution is driven by working through the use cases.

Figure 5-4: *Robustness Model–Static Model Feedback Loop*

Let's take a closer look at the three stereotypes that we apply to objects during robustness analysis.

- Boundary objects are the objects with which the actors (for instance, the users) will be interacting in the new system. These frequently include windows, screens, dialogs, and menus. If you have a GUI prototype in place, you can see what many of your primary boundary objects will be. If you follow the guidelines we gave you in Chapter 3, you can also easily pick boundary objects out of your use case text.

- Entity objects often map to the database tables and files that hold the information that needs to "outlive" use case execution. Some of your entity objects are "transient" objects, such as search results, that "die" when the use case ends. Many of your entity objects will come from your domain model.

- Control objects (controllers) embody much of the application logic. They serve as the connecting tissue between the users and the stored data. This is where you capture your frequently changing business rules and policies, with the idea that you can *localize changes* to these objects without disrupting your user interface or your database schema down the line. Once in a while (perhaps 20 percent of the time), controllers are "real objects" in a design, but most of the time, *controllers serve as placeholders to make sure that you don't forget any functionality and system behavior required by your use cases.*

You perform robustness analysis for a use case by walking through the use case text, one sentence at a time, and drawing the actor(s), the appropriate boundary and entity objects and controllers, and the connections among the various elements of the diagram. You should be able to fit the basic course and all of the alternate courses on one diagram.

Four basic rules apply:

1. Actors can only talk to boundary objects.
2. Boundary objects can only talk to controllers and actors.
3. Entity objects can only talk to controllers.
4. Controllers can talk to boundary objects, entity objects, and other controllers, but not to actors.

Keep in mind that both boundary objects and entity objects are nouns, and that controllers are verbs. Nouns can't talk to other nouns, but verbs can talk to either nouns or verbs.

Figure 5-5 summarizes the robustness diagram rules.

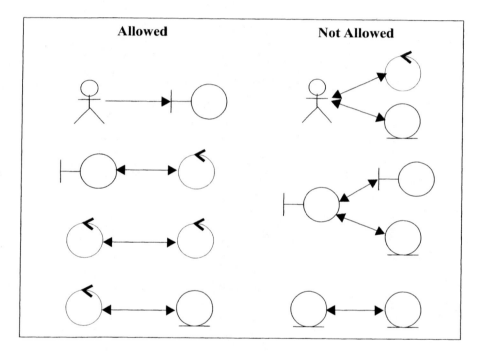

Figure 5-5: *Robustness Diagram Rules*

A reviewer of a robustness diagram should be able to read a course of action in the use case text, trace his or her finger along the associations on the diagram, and see a clear match between text and picture. You will probably have to rewrite your use case text as you do this, to remove ambiguity and to explicitly reference boundary objects and entity objects. Most people don't write perfect use case text in the first draft.

In addition to using the results of robustness analysis to tighten up the use case text, you should also continuously refine your static model. The new objects you discover drawing the diagrams should become part of your class diagrams when you discover them. This is also the right time to add some key attributes to your more significant classes.

The Top 10 Robustness Analysis Errors

The flip side of the principles we just discussed takes the form of a number of common errors that we have seen students make when they're doing robustness analysis on their projects for the first time. Our "Top 10" list follows.

Violate one or more of the noun/verb robustness diagram rules.

These rules are in place primarily to get your text into noun-verb-noun format and to help ensure that you don't start allocating behavior to objects before you have enough information to make good design decisions. (We'll talk more about behavior allocation in Chapter 7, which focuses on sequence diagrams.) The rules about boundary objects are in place to ensure that you explicitly specify the boundaries of the system, outside of which reside the actor(s) involved in your use cases.

Don't use robustness analysis to help you use a consistent format for your use case text.

The boundary object–controller–entity object pattern will tend to appear on many of your robustness diagrams. This pattern has a close correlation with the subject-verb-object pattern of basic English sentences. You should use robustness analysis to make the text of your use cases stylistically consistent among themselves to the largest extent that you can, which will greatly improve their readability and maintainability.

Don't include alternate courses on robustness diagrams.

You need to perform robustness analysis on *all* of your use case text, not just the basic courses. Much of the interesting behavior of a system occurs in the context of alternate courses, so it's very important to analyze that behavior as part of your modeling efforts. Robustness analysis can also help you discover new alternate courses, especially when you draw controllers with labels such as Verify and Validate.

Don't use robustness analysis to ensure consistency between class names on class diagrams and in use case text.

Specifying *system usage in the context of the object model* is the magic formula you need to build useful sequence diagrams. By naming your boundary objects and entity objects in your use cases, you take a healthy step toward getting your sequence diagrams off to a good start, by simply drawing those objects across the top of the sequence diagram for each use case.

Allocate behavior to classes on your robustness diagrams.

As we mentioned earlier, controllers serve as placeholders for functionality and system behavior. You should *not* start assigning methods to classes on a robustness diagram because you're not likely to have enough information just yet. You'll make decisions about behavior allocation using sequence diagrams.

Include too few or two many controllers.

We recommend having between two and five controllers on a robustness diagram. If you only have one controller per use case, you're likely to have a lot of very small use cases, each of which doesn't really describe enough behavior. On the other hand, if you have more than ten controllers on one diagram, you should consider splitting your use case up into more manageable chunks.

Take too much time trying to perfect robustness diagrams.

The robustness diagram serves as something of a "booster-stage engine" that gets the process of driving use cases forward into an object-oriented design off the ground. Robustness analysis is a tool that helps us discover objects, allocate attributes, and check the use case text for completeness and correctness. But once we've accomplished the overall mission, we don't need to maintain the work product. It's a means to an end, not an end in itself.

Try to do detailed design on robustness diagrams.

The concept of throwaway diagrams is useful in connection with preliminary design; it is *not* a useful concept when it comes to detailed design. Sequence diagrams are the appropriate place for detailed design. Robustness analysis should be *a quick pass across all of the scenarios* you're going to build, in order to provide maximum value to your project. If your preliminary design takes as long as detailed design, you'll lose the benefits of this quick sanity check.

Don't perform a visual trace between the use case text and the robustness diagram.

We strongly recommend that you have peer review of all of your use case text and robustness diagrams, with each reviewer performing the finger trace technique that we described earlier. *You should not consider your use case done until you can pass the simple visual trace test.* When you've reached the point where all of your use cases pass the test, the next step—drawing sequence diagrams—will be easier for you to perform than if you were starting from first-draft, vague, ambiguous, abstract use case text alone.

Don't update your static model.

You *must* update your domain model before you can consider yourself done with robustness analysis and ready to move on to interaction modeling using sequence diagrams. You can't allocate behavior to classes that don't appear in your static model, after all.

Exercises

The following exercises, which come from the robustness diagrams within the model for our Internet Bookstore, are designed to test your ability to spot the top 10 mistakes that people make during robustness analysis. Each page with a red label at the top contains three or four of these mistakes; your task is to write corrections on the page near the erroneous material. Following each of these pages is a page with a white label inside a black box at the top; this page contains corrected material and explanations of the top 10 rules that were violated on the previous page. Happy hunting!

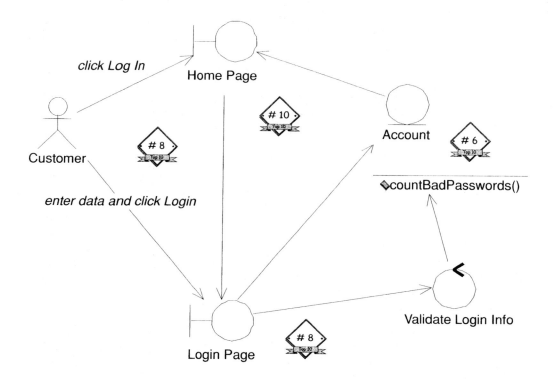

Log In

click Log In

Home Page

10

Customer

8

Account

6

◆countBadPasswords()

enter data and click Login

Validate Login Info

Login Page

8

Basic Course: The Customer clicks the Log In button on the Home Page. The system displays the Login Page. The Customer enters his or her user ID and password and then clicks the Log In button. The system validates the login information against the persistent Account data and then returns the Customer to the Home Page.

Alternate Courses:

If the Customer clicks the New Account button on the Login Page, the system invokes the Open Account use case. If the Customer clicks the Reminder Word button on the Login Page, the system displays the reminder word stored for that Customer, in a separate dialog box. When the Customer clicks the OK button, the system returns the Customer to the Login Page.

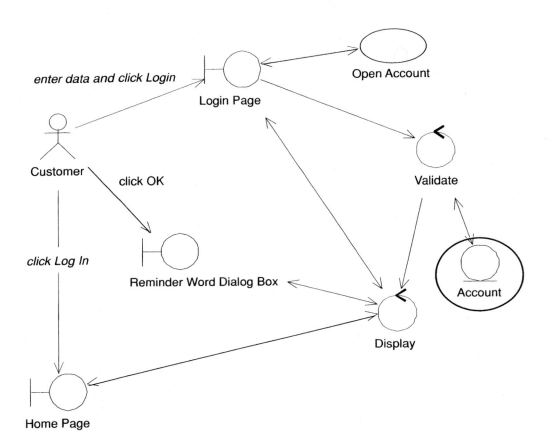

On the previous diagram:

- The HomePage boundary object talked to the Login Page boundary object and the Account entity object.
- The Account object had a method assigned to it.
- No alternate courses were represented.

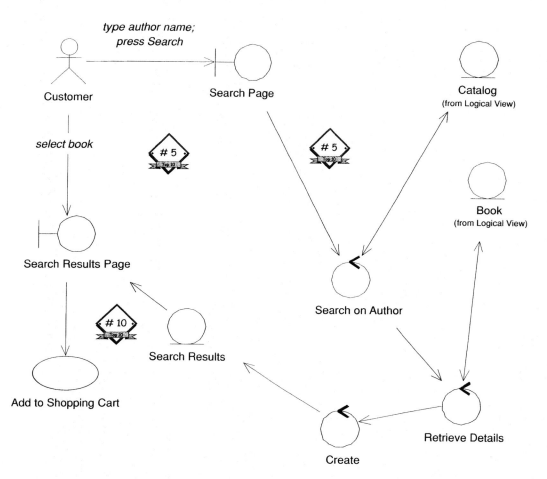

Search by Author

type author name;
press Search

Customer

Search Page

Catalog
(from Logical View)

select book

5
Top 10

5
Top 10

Book
(from Logical View)

Search Results Page

Search on Author

10
Top 10

Search Results

Add to Shopping Cart

Create

Retrieve Details

Basic Course: The Customer types the name of an Author on the Search Page and then presses the Search button. The system ensures that the Customer typed a valid search phrase, Author and then searches the Catalog and retrieves all of the Books with which that is associated. The the system retrieves the important details about each Book.

2
Top 10

Then the system displays the list of Books on the Search Results Page, with the Books listed in reverse chronological order by publication date. Each entry has a thumbnail of the Book's cover, the Book's title and authors, the average Rating, and an Add to Shopping Cart button. The Customer presses the Add to Shopping Cart button for a particular Book. The system passes control to the Add Item to Shopping Cart use case.

Alternate Courses:…no search phrase…no books found…Customer exits before searching…

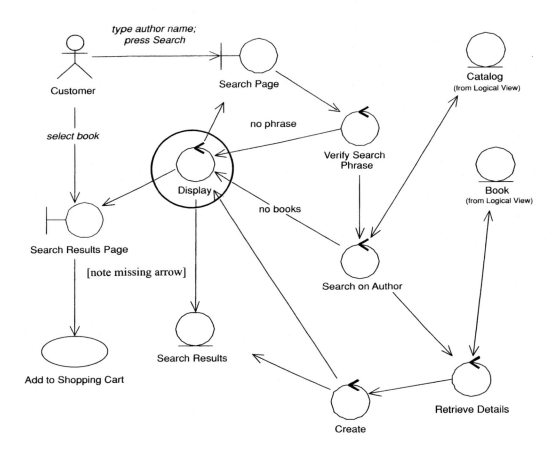

The sytstem retrieves the important details about each Book *and creates Search Results with that information.* Then the system displays the list of Books on the Search Results Page....

On the previous diagram:

- There are too few controllers. Verify Search Phrase enables the system to avoid performing a search with no search phrase, while Display is a standard controller associated with Web pages. (These controllers also reflect alternate courses that the previous diagram didn't.)

- The Search Results entity object is talking to the Search Results Page boundary object.

- The use case text doesn't reflect the creation of the Search Results object.

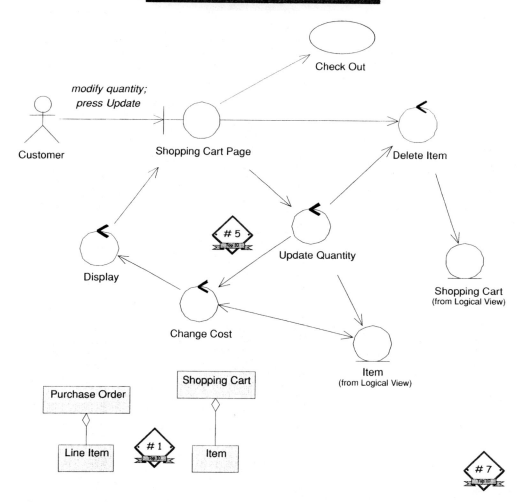

Edit Contents of Shopping Cart

Basic Course: On the Shopping Cart Page, the Customer modifies the quantity of a Line Item in the Shopping Cart and then presses the Update button. The system stores the new quantity and then computes and displays the new cost for that Line Item. The Customer Presses the Continue Shopping button. The system returns control to the use case from which it received control.

Alternate Courses: (1) If the Customer changes the quantity of the Item to 0, the system deletes that Item from the Shopping Cart. (2) If the Customer presses the Delete button instead of the Update button, the system deletes that Item from the Shopping Cart. (3) If the Customer presses the Check Out button instead of the Continue Shopping button, the system passes control to the Check Out use case.

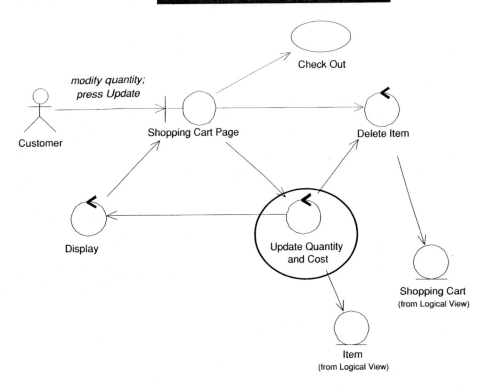

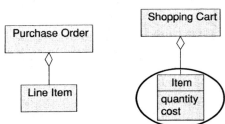

On the Shopping Cart Page, the Customer modifies the quantity of *an Item* in the Shopping Cart, then presses the Update button. The system stores the new quantity, then computes and displays the new cost for that *Item*.

On the previous diagram:

- The Change Cost controller is unnecessary, since both it and the Update Quantity controller operate on the Item object.
- The use case text refers to Line Item, but it's clear from the class diagram excerpt and the robustness diagram that the text should refer to Item instead. (This kind of name usage inconsistency can be deadly.)
- The class diagram excerpt doesn't reflect the attributes that are mentioned in the use case text.

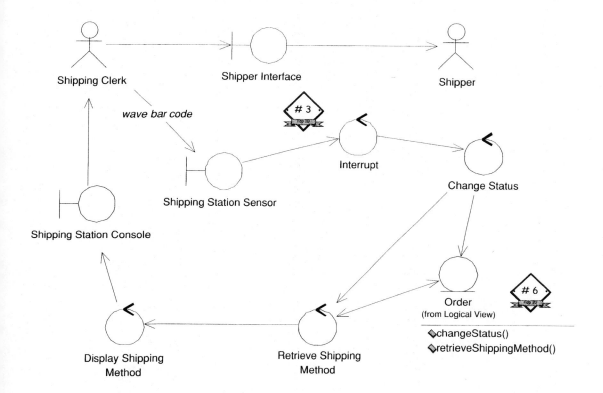

Basic Course: The Shipping Clerk ensures that the Items listed on the packing slip for the Order match the physical items. The Clerk waves the bar code on the packing slip under the sensor at the shipping station. The status of the order is changed to "shipping." The Shipping Method is displayed on the Shipping Station Console.

The Clerk weighs the set of physical items. The Clerk packages the Items. The Clerk attaches a manifest appropriate for the given shipping method. The Clerk waves the bar code on the manifest under the sensor. The Clerk sends the package out via the associated Shipper.

Alternate Course: If the Shipping Clerk finds a mismatch between the Order and the physical items, the Clerk stops processing of the Order until he or she is able to make a match.

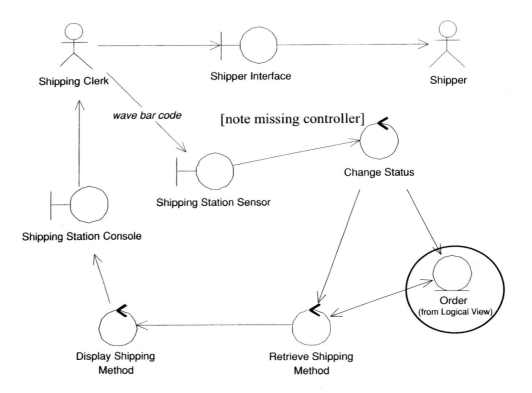

The system changes the status of the Order to "shipping." Then the system retrieves the Shipping Method that the Customer specified for this Order and displays it on the Shpping Station Console.

On the previous diagram:

- The Interrupt object is a construct that belongs to detailed design.
- The Order object had methods assigned to it.
- The use case text is in passive voice and not as precise as it should be relative to the robustness diagram.

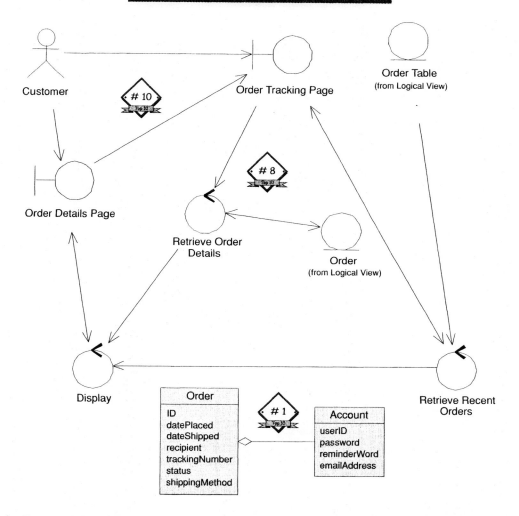

Take Recent Orders

Basic Course: The system retrieves the Orders that the Customer has placed within the last 30 days and displays these Orders on the Order Tracking Page. Each entry has the Order ID (in the form of a link), the Order date, the Order status, the Order recipient, and the Shipping Method by which the Order was shipped. The Customer clicks on a link. The system retrieves the relevant contents of the Order, and then displays that information, in view-only mode, on the Order Details Page. The Customer presses OK to return to the Order Tracking Page. Once the Customer has finished viewing Orders, he or she clicks the Account Maintenance link on the Order Tracking Page. The system returns control to the invoking use case.

Alternate Course: If the Customer has not placed any Orders within the last 30 days, the system displays a message to that effect on the Order Tracking Page.

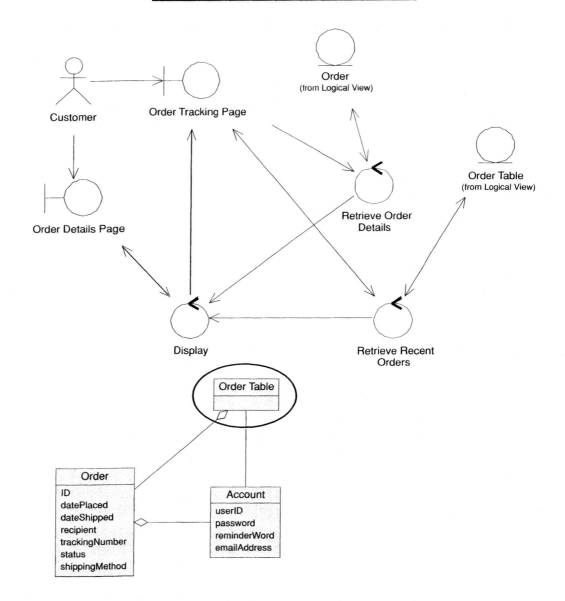

On the previous diagram:

- The Order Details Page boundary object is talking to the Order Tracking Page boundary object.
- There's no indication of what happens if the Customer hasn't placed any recent orders.
- The class diagram excerpt doesn't reflect the (newly discovered) Order Table class.

Bringing the Pieces Together

Figure 5-6 shows the class diagram that includes some of the attributes on the classes for our Internet Bookstore.

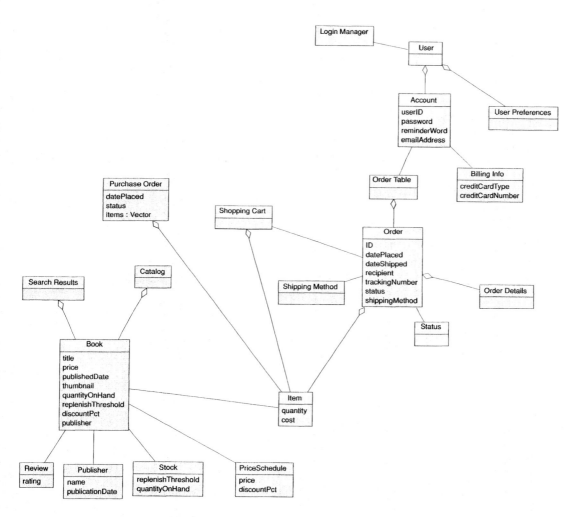

Figure 5-6: *Domain Model with Attributes for The Internet Bookstore*

Chapter 6

Preliminary Design Review

Preliminary design review (PDR) involves reviewing the robustness diagrams and use case text for each scenario you're planning to build, and making sure that the diagrams and the use case text match each other and that both are complete and correctly represent the desired system behavior. It also involves ensuring that the domain model matches the robustness diagrams—in particular, that all entity objects that show up on robustness diagrams are represented in the domain model. In other words, we verify that we've identified the key abstractions from the problem space that we'll need to implement the desired behavior.

We should also review to make sure these entity classes are populated with attributes and that we can trace data flow between the screens of our system (which should now have names) through our entity classes, and perhaps into some underlying database tables where we have persistent data. We should also be reviewing the technical architecture behind our evolving design and making sure that the design we're beginning to develop is plausible in the context of that technical architecture.

Figure 6-1 shows where we are.

The Key Elements of Preliminary Design Review

PDR should involve representatives of both the customer(s) and the development team, as well as any necessary managers, just like requirements review. There's a key difference, though: this is the last chance for the customer to change requirements before the developers drive the given set of use cases through to code. You can think of PDR as representing a line beyond which customers are no longer welcome to actively participate in the process. We talked previously about how use cases represent contracts between customers and developers; it's during PDR that you finalize those contracts.

As we described in Chapter 5, robustness analysis provides a *sanity check* by helping you make sure that your use case text is correct and that you haven't specified system behavior that's unreasonable—or impossible—given the set of objects you have to work with.

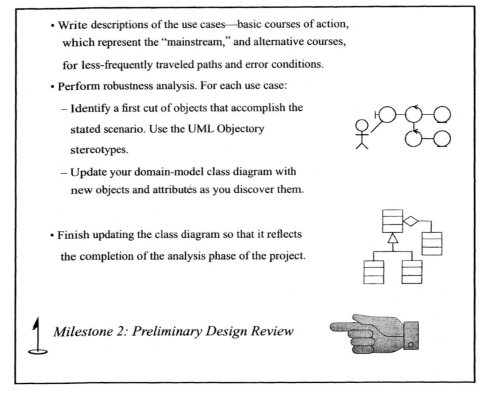

- Write descriptions of the use cases—basic courses of action, which represent the "mainstream," and alternative courses, for less-frequently traveled paths and error conditions.
- Perform robustness analysis. For each use case:
  - Identify a first cut of objects that accomplish the stated scenario. Use the UML Objectory stereotypes.
  - Update your domain-model class diagram with new objects and attributes as you discover them.

- Finish updating the class diagram so that it reflects the completion of the analysis phase of the project.

Milestone 2: Preliminary Design Review

Figure 6-1: *Preliminary Design Review and the ICONIX Process*

This refinement of the use case text changes the nature of that text from a pure user manual perspective to a usage description *in the context of the object model*. PDR should center around peer review of all use case text and robustness diagrams. Each reviewer should be able to do the following for each use case.

- Read the course of action.
- Trace his or her finger along the associations on the corresponding robustness diagram.
- See a clear match between text and picture.

Figure 5-5 shows the rules of robustness analysis. Given that both boundary objects and entity objects are nouns, and that controllers are verbs, we can see that nouns can't talk to other nouns, but verbs can talk to either nouns or verbs. The goal is to *itemize all the required behavior of the use case* in the form of control objects (controllers). This involves taking the user manual view and identifying all the logical functions that must occur, then massaging the narrative of the use case text into a straightforward noun-verb-noun format. This format will allow us to *check for correctness* when we embark upon detailed design by ensuring that we don't forget any behavior while we're doing the design. Doing this also helps enforce a common noun-verb-noun style of writing use cases across a design team.

As we just mentioned, the verbs in your use case text are represented as controllers on your robustness diagrams. These controllers encapsulate the control flow, and they serve as the "glue" between boundary objects and entity objects, between boundaries and other boundaries, and between entities and other entities. Remember that the reason we call them controllers, rather than control objects, is that they serve as *placeholders*—we're not ready to assign the behavior they represent to any objects yet because we don't have enough information. Decisions about which methods go on which boundary objects and entity objects, and also about which controllers deserve to become full objects in your static model, are premature; we make them during sequence diagramming, *not* on robustness diagrams.

Arrows can go in one or both directions between different types of objects on a robustness diagram. An arrow pointing from a boundary object to a control object indicates that the former is signaling the latter to perform. Or there might be a two-headed arrow between a control object and an entity object, signifying that they read from each other and write to each other. Note, however, that you need to use only one type of arrowhead, which is *not* the case on several types of UML diagrams. Unlike arrows on sequence diagrams, arrows on robustness diagrams *don't* represent software messages; rather, they simply indicate communication associations. Because you won't code from these diagrams, focus on the logical flow of your use case and worry about the directions of arrows later, in your sequence diagrams.

You should, however, be aware of the presence of patterns across robustness diagrams. Patterns often start becoming visible during robustness analysis. There are two strategies, "control in the screen" and "use case controller," that lend themselves to discovering patterns connected to use cases. (See *Use Case Driven Object Modeling* for details about these terms.) Looking ahead to interaction modeling, design patterns can be highly useful in the context of sequence diagrams and design-level class diagrams. You should *not*, though, start drawing full design patterns on your robustness diagrams; it's sufficient to start thinking about how you'll be able to use them to advantage during detailed design.

We used the term **technical architecture** at the beginning of the chapter. This refers to the set of basic decisions you need to make about what technologies you're going to use in implementing the system. These decisions involve things such as the programming language (for instance, Java versus Visual Basic) and how you're going to build and distribute software components (will you go with Enterprise Java Beans [EJBs] and Java Server Pages [JSPs], or take the Microsoft route with Distributed Component Object Model [DCOM] components and Active Server Pages [ASPs]?). The decisions you make about your technical architecture need to be reflected, to some extent, on your robustness diagrams.

If, for instance, you're building with a technical architecture that involves EJBs and JSPs, your robustness diagrams will tend to reflect the "control in the screen" pattern more than they would if you were building pure HTML pages. Thus, robustness analysis, which is meant to give you a loose description of the design that you can crank out quickly, offers the chance for you to verify that your technical architecture works for the scenarios you're building, and your review of these diagrams becomes a "do-ability" check on that architecture.

Continuing the thought about patterns: The concept of throwaway diagrams is useful in connection with preliminary design; it is *not* a useful concept when it comes to detailed design. Sequence diagrams are the appropriate place for detailed design. Robustness analysis should be a quick pass across all of the scenarios you're going to build, in order to provide maximum value to your project. If your preliminary design takes as long as detailed design, you'll lose the benefits of this quick sanity check.

Robustness analysis allows you to make a reuse pass through the entire use case model before you commit any use cases to the design. Looking for reuse possibilities also helps you identify objects you missed during domain modeling. You *must* update your static model before you can consider yourself done with robustness analysis and ready to move on to interaction modeling (the subject of Chapter 7). The new objects you discovered while you were drawing all those robustness diagrams and talking about them with your customers need to go onto your class diagrams *now*, not later.

This is also the right time to add some key attributes to your more significant classes. While we're talking about attributes: As we introduce windows and screens—in the form of boundary objects—to our robustness diagrams, we begin to *trace data* associated with those objects back to the entity objects from which the data comes and/or to which it goes. The natural result of that tracing is the *addition of attributes* to the classes in the domain model.

The Top 10 PDR Errors

The flip side of the principles we just discussed takes the form of a number of common errors that our students make when they're doing preliminary design review for their projects. Our "Top 10" list follows.

Don't make sure the customers know that this is their last chance to change the behavior before this release of the system is built.

Robustness analysis is where use cases get tightened up and the development team gets ready to jump into detailed design. Your goal should be to have iron-clad use cases in place before you start drawing sequence diagrams. As such, customers need to sign off on those use cases during PDR. If you let customers continue to monkey with use cases after this review, you increase the risk of "feature creep," and you're also likely to run into problems with trying to do a design while the requirements are changing underfoot.

Don't make sure the use case text and robustness diagrams match.

A reviewer of a robustness diagram should be able to read a course of action in the use case text, trace his or her finger along the associations on the diagram, and see a clear match between text and picture. If the reviewer can't do this, you need to rewrite your use case text, redo your diagram, or both. You should *not* proceed with a sequence diagram for the given use case without passing this simple test because your use case isn't done if it doesn't pass, and therefore, you're not going to be able to do good detailed design for it. We're fond of calling this process **disambiguation**. This involves removing the ambiguity from your use case text. We'd all rather not design against ambiguous requirements if we can avoid it.

Don't make sure that new entity objects are added to the domain model.

One of the reasons to do robustness analysis is to accelerate the evolution of the initial (problem space) domain model toward a final (solution space) class model. You build that final class model by allocating behavior to all of the objects that come into play within your use cases. You can't do behavior allocation properly if you don't have all of your classes represented within your static model before you start drawing sequence diagrams.

Don't look for attributes on the domain classes.

You should strive to have a pretty full and rich set of attributes on the classes in your domain model when you're through with robustness analysis for a given set of use cases. As we mentioned earlier, a number of these attributes should match up with elements of your boundary objects, such as fields on a window or screen. Other attributes will be more relevant to functionality that's internal to the system. If you don't capture these attributes before you start doing sequence diagrams, your decisions about which class does which operation will be less informed than they should be. When we do OO design, we generally put the functions where the data is. However, within our approach, we make these decisions in two steps: We start allocating data during preliminary design, and we revisit this allocation when we allocate the functions, during detailed design.

Expect operations to be allocated to classes during PDR.

As we discussed in Chapter 5, controllers serve as *placeholders* for functionality and system behavior. You should *not* start assigning methods to classes on a robustness diagram because you're not likely to have enough information just yet. You'll make decisions about behavior allocation using sequence diagrams, as we describe in Chapter 7.

Don't advise your customers (again) that use case text is a contract between developers and clients.

We tell you in Chapter 7 that you should copy the use case text onto the sequence diagram you'll be drawing for that use case. The result of this is that *when you're doing the design, the required system behavior is always staring you in the face.* This reinforces, to the designers, the nature of use cases as contracts between customers and developers. It's during PDR that you have to reinforce that principle to your customers.

Require the preliminary static design to make extensive use of design patterns.

We talked about the concept of premature patternization in Chapter 2. This is also a trap that people tend to fall into during robustness analysis and PDR. It's healthy to discover patterns across robustness diagrams, especially those that map easily to established design patterns or patterns that you've invented. What's not healthy is expanding simple preliminary design patterns that appear on robustness diagrams into detailed design patterns. Save the latter for sequence diagrams and design-level class diagrams.

Don't review the noun/verb rules of robustness analysis.

On a sequence diagram, it's perfectly acceptable for nouns to talk to other nouns—this is because the verbs represent the messages between objects—so boundary objects can talk to other boundaries, entity objects to other entities, boundaries to entities. On a robustness diagram, though, nouns only talk to verbs, not other nouns. The associated rules are in place to help you ensure that your use case is expressed correctly, in noun-verb-noun format just like standard English dictates, because we need to have both the nouns and the verbs identified before we draw our sequence diagrams. Consistency of your use case text across the project helps ensure a fairly straightforward move into sequence diagramming as you continue to use your use cases to drive your design.

Expect your robustness diagrams to show a complete detailed design rather than a conceptual design.

We've already told you that you shouldn't see methods or design patterns on your diagrams, so you shouldn't be surprised that we're going to tell you that you should *not* be exploring any other facets of detailed design when you're doing PDR. Also, use cases, class diagrams, and sequence diagrams are persistent; robustness diagrams aren't (at least, not necessarily; a lot of folks like to keep them around, especially if they're contained within a visual model, and there's nothing wrong with this). So, you shouldn't waste time trying to perfect your robustness diagrams as your design evolves.

Review the direction of every arrow on a robustness diagram carefully instead of doing a quick trace to verify you've accounted for all of the behavior.

Robustness analysis is meant to be a "quick and dirty" technique that helps you tighten up your use cases, discover new objects, and get a good start toward detailed design. Robustness diagrams are meant as a means to an end; it's a waste of time to make the effort to get the arrows exactly right. You should focus your efforts on perfecting your sequence diagrams rather than tinkering with robustness diagrams.

Chapter 7

Sequence Diagrams

After we finish our robustness diagrams and have a preliminary design review, it's time to move forward into detailed design. Robustness analysis—preliminary design—is about object discovery. Detailed design is largely about allocating behavior: allocating the software functions we have identified into the set of objects that we have discovered. In this chapter, we focus on the sequence diagram as the central element of detailed design, or at least of the dynamic part of our object model.

Once we're through doing preliminary design using robustness analysis, we'll go back through our scenarios and do a second, more detailed pass through the design. We're going to take another look at our informal first guesses at how these objects collaborate together and make those statements very precise. By the time we get to this point of the project, we should have accomplished two things. First, our use case text should now be very complete, correct, detailed, and explicit. Second, we should have discovered most of the objects that we're going to need in the system, at least at a conceptual, or idealized, level of abstraction.

Figure 7-1 shows where sequence diagrams reside within the "big picture" for the ICONIX process.

The Key Elements of Sequence Diagrams

You want to achieve three primary goals during interaction modeling.

- *Allocate behavior among boundary, entity, and control objects.* During robustness analysis, you identify (or at least take an educated guess at) a set of objects that together could accomplish the desired behavior of our use cases. You also break that behavior down into discrete units and create placeholder control objects for each of those units of behavior. Now you need to decide which objects are responsible for which bits of behavior. If you are not certain about what the relevant boundary, entity, and control objects are, it's too soon to be contemplating how you will allocate behavior. Go back to robustness analysis and make sure.

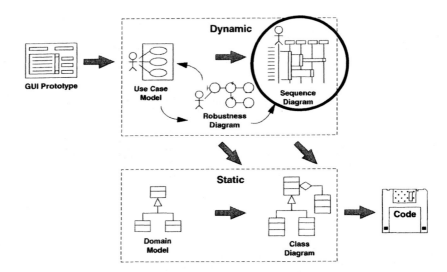

Figure 7-1: *Sequence Diagrams Drive the Allocation of Behavior to Software Classes*

- *Show the detailed interactions that occur over time among the objects associated with each of your use cases.* Objects interact at runtime by sending messages to each other. These messages serve as what Jacobson calls stimuli—that is, a message stimulates an object to perform some desired action. For each unit of behavior within a use case, you must identify the necessary messages/methods.

- *Finalize the distribution of operations among classes.* You should aim to have a fairly high percentage (perhaps 75 or 80 percent) of your attributes defined within the static model when you finish with robustness analysis. We advocate a minimalist approach to defining operations during domain modeling and robustness analysis. In fact, we recommend that you don't assign *any* methods during preliminary design. That's because there isn't enough information available with which to make good design decisions about operations at that stage of a project. (Think about it: You haven't discovered all of the objects until you've completed all of your robustness diagrams, and trying to allocate behavior into an incomplete set of objects is going to be error-prone at best.) When you get to interaction modeling, however, you do have good information (at least you hope to). As you lay out the detailed behavior of your objects, on sequence diagrams, in the context of your use cases, you should begin to finalize the process of finding appropriate homes for attributes and operations. While you do this *dynamic* modeling, you will be updating and expanding your *static* model, which will solidify your increasing knowledge of how your new system should work.

The UML's **sequence diagram** evolved from Jacobson's object interaction diagram and the event trace diagram from OMT. Within the ICONIX approach, *sequence diagrams represent the major work product of design*. You draw one sequence diagram that encompasses the basic course and *all alternate courses of action* within each of your use cases. (You can use more than one page if you need to.) The results form the core of your dynamic model, in which the behavior of your system at runtime, including *how* the system will accomplish that behavior, is defined in great detail.

There are four types of elements on a sequence diagram.

- *The text for the course of action of the use case* appears down the left-hand side. It's a good idea to break up the text with white space so that it's easy to see which sentence(s) correspond with each set of elements to the right.

- *Objects*, which you bring over directly from your robustness diagrams, are represented in rectangular boxes with two names. The name or instance number, and the name of the object's class, appear in the form object:class. Either name can be omitted. The objects can optionally be displayed with their robustness diagram stereotypes; this is often helpful in keeping track of messages passed among actors, boundary objects, and entity objects.

- *Messages* are arrows between objects. A message arrow can go directly between two dotted lines, between a line and a method rectangle, or between two method rectangles (see below).

- *Methods (operations)* are shown as rectangles that lie on top of the dotted lines that belong to the objects to which you're assigning the methods. You can use the lengths of these rectangles to reflect the *focus of control* within the sequence: a particular method is in control up to the point at which its rectangle ends. Unfortunately, focus of control is often more useful in theory than in practice, because most visual modeling tools aren't very well-behaved with respect to this particular feature. If you find yourself getting frustrated with trying to show focus of control on your diagrams, don't hesitate to just turn its display off—you don't want anything to distract you from making good behavior allocation decisions.

Getting Started with Sequence Diagrams

It's been our experience that many people get stuck at this point in a development project. (This is especially likely if they've skipped preliminary design.) The technique we describe below evolved from helping students get "unstuck" during dozens of training workshops over the past several years.

Figure 7-2 shows the four steps you perform when drawing sequence diagrams the ICONIX way.

1. *Copy the text for the given use case from the use case specification.* Paste it onto the left margin of the page. Copying use case text to begin the corresponding sequence diagram enables that text to serve as an ongoing reminder of what you're trying to accomplish. The result of this is that *when you're doing the design, the required system behavior is always staring you in the face.* Note that if you don't have all the relevant alternative courses of action written out for each of your use cases, you should *not* proceed with your sequence diagram. The diagrams will not cover all special cases, and you will not uncover all the behavior of the use case. *This means that you won't discover all of the necessary methods for your objects.* (Do Not Pass GO; Do Not Collect $200.)

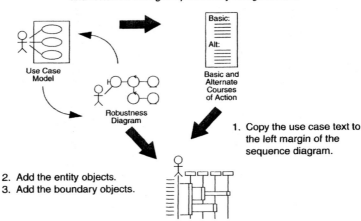

Figure 7-2: *Building a Sequence Diagram*

2. *Add the entity objects* from the robustness diagram. Each of these objects is an instance of a class that appears on the class diagram that represents your static model. (If you forgot to update your static class diagrams in response to new objects discovered during robustness analysis, *do it now.* These objects should have most of their attributes in place. Many of them will be serving data to other objects.) You can expect to discover missing attributes as you work through your sequence diagram. Be religious about adding them to your static model; this is likely to be your last step before code.

3. *Add the boundary objects* and actors from the robustness diagram. We didn't mention adding boundary objects to your domain model because these objects are part of the solution space; the domain model addresses the problem space. By accounting for boundary objects on your sequence diagrams, you begin integrating the two spaces at the start of detailed design.

If you follow the ICONIX approach, the first three steps in drawing sequence diagrams are completely mechanical in nature. (In fact, we've reduced them to an executable script that automatically generates a skeleton of a sequence diagram. If you use Rational Rose, you can download a copy of this script from **http://www.iconixsw.com/RoseScripts.html**. Similar functionality is becoming available for other tools, such as GDPro from Embarcadero and Together/J from TogetherSoft.) Scripts such as this have proven to be very useful in achieving momentum as you get serious about your design. You get an immediate payback in time savings from the work you invested in your robustness diagrams, which can be very useful as you get serious about your design. The fourth step, deciding which methods go on which classes, is the essence of interaction modeling.

Putting methods on classes involves *converting the controllers* from your robustness diagram, one at a time, to sets of methods and messages that embody the desired behavior. (Occasionally, you might elect to turn a controller into a real control object.) Along these lines, we suggest that you *use your robustness diagram as a checklist* to make sure you have all the required system behavior accounted for on your sequence diagrams. You simply check off each control object as you draw the corresponding message(s) on the sequence diagrams. This will help you eliminate the "oops, I forgot about that function" error—which, as you might guess, is an insidious one. (Note that one controller on a robustness diagram can translate to several methods on a sequence diagram.)

There are two basic strategies for converting the controllers from your robustness diagrams: "control in the screen" and "use case controller." If you were to head consistently in one or the other direction during your sequence diagramming efforts across all of your use cases, that would qualify as patternizing. The idea is that the team members who are responsible for the diagrams should establish, early in this task, some design standards that can be used across all your use cases.

Looking in another direction: As you're diagramming the interactions among the various objects, well-established design patterns, such as those you might find in the Gang of Four book (Erich Gamma, Richard Helm, Ralph Johnson, and John Vlissides: *Design Patterns*, Addison-Wesley, 1995) would fit in nicely. Or perhaps you might develop new patterns to establish a standardized approach to design problems that appear across multiple use cases. Now is the time to visit your static model and reflect those design decisions on your class diagrams, then draw your sequence diagrams to match. This is where much of real object-oriented design (OOD) takes place.

You've already checked the robustness diagrams against your use case text. By checking your sequence diagrams against your robustness diagrams, you add a measure of assurance that *you're designing in response to what the user needs* (in other words, meeting your requirements).

The Top 10 Sequence Diagramming Errors

The flip side of the principles we just discussed takes the form of a number of common errors that we have seen students make when they're drawing sequence diagrams on their projects for the first time. Our "Top 10" list follows.

Don't do a sequence diagram for each use case.

Jacobson provided a straightforward description of the need for interaction modeling in his business process reengineering (BPR) book (*The Object Advantage*, Addison-Wesley, 1995): "It is only after you have drawn interaction diagrams [called "sequence diagrams" in the UML] for all courses of events in all use cases that you can be certain that you have found all of the roles that the system requires each object to play and, thus, the responsibilities of each object."

Don't put the use case text on the sequence diagram.

Writing the original requirements-level text for the use case (after "disambiguation" of that text as a result of robustness analysis) in the margin of the sequence diagram provides visual requirements traceability from the design back to your user-certified requirements. The project team will have put a lot of effort into writing the use case text, and the user community should have signed off on the results. The diagram should match the narrative flow of the associated use case.

Don't identify all of the necessary objects first, on a robustness diagram.

If you're having trouble getting a sequence diagram started, you probably wrote the use case incorrectly and/or didn't complete robustness analysis. Having proper robustness diagrams, associated with rigorously defined use cases, in place makes the job significantly easier.

Don't provide a visual trace between the use case text and the message arrows.

Each sentence, and each sentence fragment as appropriate, within the use case text should have some white space around it, and each sentence or fragment should line up visually with the message or set of messages that correspond with the specified behavior. This will enable people reading the diagram to easily see *how* the system will accomplish the *what* that the use case describes.

Don't show plumbing; instead, keep your sequence diagram at a high level of abstraction.

It isn't necessary to show plumbing on robustness diagrams, since they reflect a preliminary design view, but the sequence diagrams serve as the last stop before coding and as such need to show the real design in full detail.

Turn your sequence diagram into a flowchart instead of using it to allocate behavior among objects.

Remember that the sequence diagram is the primary vehicle for making behavior allocation decisions. You're really using your sequence diagrams to assign operations to your classes as you go, which means that you should *not* label your message arrows with free-form text, but should instead link the message name to the name of an operation on a class. (In Rational Rose, for example, you make this linkage by right-clicking the mouse on the message arrow; Rose provides visual feedback in the form of parentheses after the operation name. Behavior allocation—deciding which operations belong to which classes—is of *critical* importance in the ICONIX approach. Decisions made during this phase of a project dictate whether the overall design is good or bad. This is where experienced designers earn their pay.

Don't focus on interesting methods (real software behavior), as opposed to getters and setters.

By exploring the dynamic behavior of the system, you learn which attributes and operations are needed in the classes contained within your static model. To start, add attributes and methods to your classes as soon as you decide where they go in the context of your sequence diagrams. Note, however, that you should *not* spend much time drawing "getAttribute" and "setAttribute" message arrows on your sequence diagram. However, it's still a good idea to take advantage of the principle of encapsulation: Only allow access to attributes via "getter"s and "setter"s. You just don't have to show every "get" and "set" on your sequence diagram. This gets counterproductive because it's easy for you to lose the flow of the scenario that way.

Don't think carefully about the origins of the message arrows (in other words, which object is in control at any given time).

Messages between objects invoke the operations on the associated classes. Whereas it's not that important to get the arrows precisely right on robustness diagrams, it's *essential* that you get them right on sequence diagrams. The flow of control needs to be explicit; it should be obvious at all times which object is in control.

Don't follow basic principles of responsibility-driven OOD when allocating behavior by drawing message arrows.

An object (and, by extension, a class) should have a single "personality," and you should do your best to avoid "schizophrenic" objects. This means that a class should be focused on a strongly related set of behaviors. This parallels the well-established rules that state that objects should be highly cohesive and loosely coupled. Other principles you should focus on include reusability (the more general your objects and classes, the higher the probability that you'll be able to reuse those objects and classes for other projects) and applicability (when you assign methods to the objects on your sequence diagrams, always ask yourself whether there seems to be a good fit between method and object, and also whether the task the method performs is obviously relevant to the object.)

Don't update your static model as you go by building local class diagrams for each package of use cases.

It's nice to keep a "clean" set of domain classes on a pure domain model diagram. However, it's also a good idea to draw "localized" static class diagrams that show *both* solution space objects and problem space objects. A good guideline for this is one such diagram per package of use cases. As you come up with scaffolding and other types of infrastructure, such as "helper" classes, put them on the static class diagram, as well. This is where you shift your focus from the problem space to the solution space. It's best to use localized class diagrams—say, one per use case package—because, by this time, your static model is probably too expansive to be captured within one readable diagram. Doing this also allows work to be split across teams.

Exercises

The following exercises, which come from the sequence diagrams within the model for our Internet Bookstore, are designed to test your ability to spot the top 10 mistakes that people make during sequence diagramming. Each page with a red label at the top contains three or four of these mistakes; your task is to write corrections on the page near the erroneous material. Following each of these pages is a page with a white label inside a black box at the top; this page contains corrected material and explanations of the top 10 rules that were violated on the previous page. Happy hunting!

Search by Author

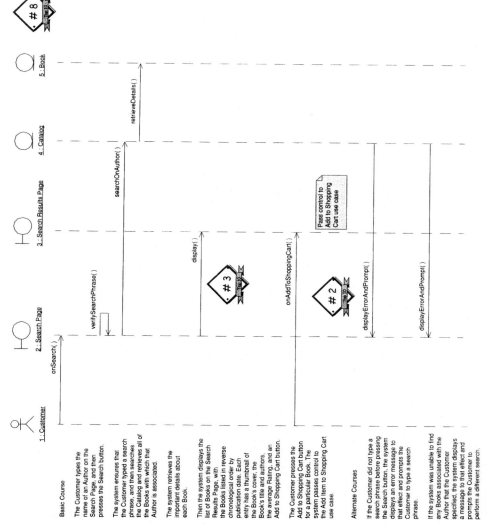

Basic Course

The Customer types the name of an Author on the Search Page, and then presses the Search button.

The system ensures that the Customer typed a search phrase, and then searches the Catalog and retrieves all of the Books with which that Author is associated.

The system retrieves the important details about each Book.

Then the system displays the list of Books on the Search Results Page, with the Books listed in reverse chronological order by publication date. Each entry has a thumbnail of the Book's cover, the Book's title and authors, the average Rating, and an Add to Shopping Cart button.

The Customer presses the Add to Shopping Cart button for a particular Book. The system passes control to the Add Item to Shopping Cart use case.

Alternate Courses

If the Customer did not type a search phrase before pressing the Search button, the system displays an error message to that effect and prompts the Customer to type a search phrase.

If the system was unable to find any Books associated with the Author that the Customer specified, the system displays a message to that effect and prompts the Customer to perform a different search.

If the Customer leaves the page in a way other than by pressing an Add to Shopping Cart button, the system returns control to the use case from which this use case received control.

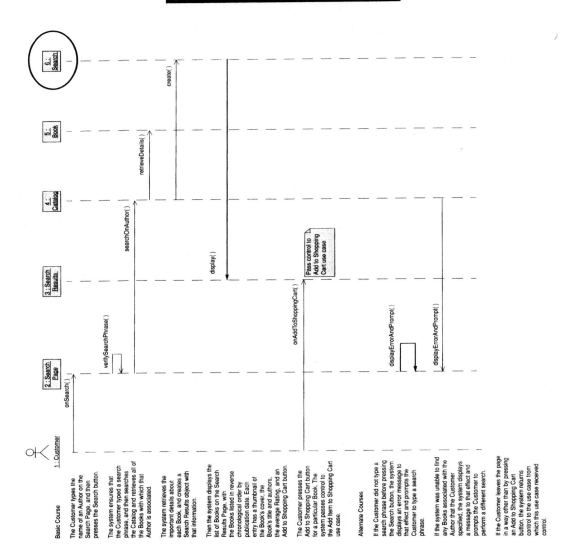

On the previous diagram:

- There is no Search Results object. This object would have been identified during robustness analysis, since we obviously aren't supposed to display the entire contents of the catalog. (Note that the case text on that diagram was incorrect as well in this regard.)

- The Search Page sent a display message even though the diagram shows that the Catalog is in control.

- The Catalog object invokes the displayErrorAndPrompt method on the Search Page.

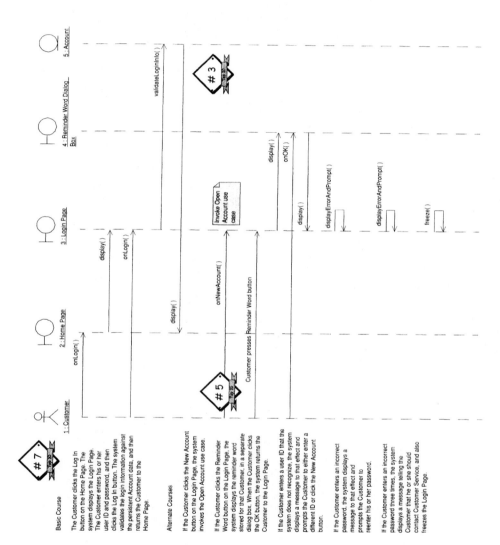

Log In

Basic Course

The Customer clicks the Log In button on the Home Page. The system displays the Login Page. The Customer enters his or her user ID and password, and then clicks the Log In button. The system validates the login information against the persistent Account data, and then returns the Customer to the Home Page.

Alternate Courses

If the Customer clicks the New Account button on the Login Page, the system invokes the Open Account use case.

If the Customer clicks the Reminder Word button on the Login Page, the system displays the reminder word stored for that Customer, in a separate dialog box. When the Customer clicks the OK button, the system returns the Customer to the Login Page.

If the Customer enters a user ID that the system does not recognize, the system displays a message to that effect and prompts the Customer to either enter a different ID or click the New Account button.

If the Customer enters an incorrect password, the system displays a message to that effect and prompts the Customer to reenter his or her password.

If the Customer enters an incorrect password three times, the system displays a message telling the Customer that he or she should contact Customer Service, and also freezes the Login Page.

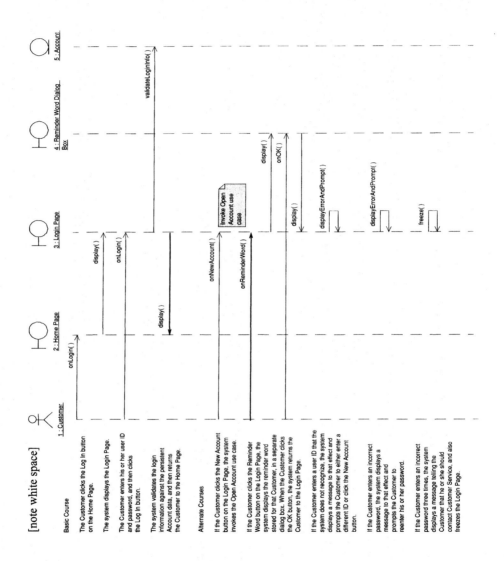

On the previous diagram:

- The use case test doesn't line up visually with the message arrows.

- The Account object sent a display message even though the diagram shows that the Login Page is in control.

- The arrow associated with the "reminder word" alternate course has a label, rather than behavior allocation in the form of a method.

Ship Order

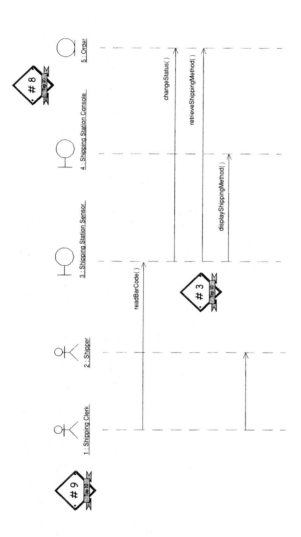

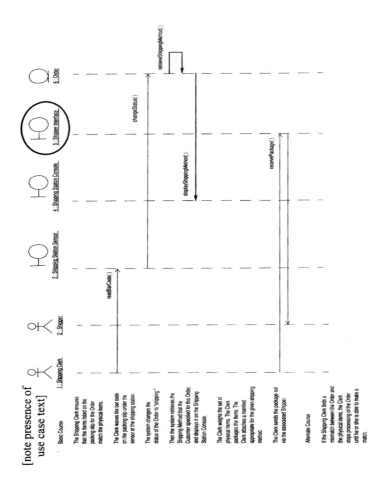

Ship Order

On the previous diagram:

- The use case text doesn't appear on the left side.
- The Shipper Interface is missing; the fact that the Shipping Clerk talks directly to the Shipper means that the diagram doesn't show how the shipment gets recorded.
- The Sensor object has control, even though this isn't logical for a sensor in this kind of situation.

Edit Contents of Shopping Cart

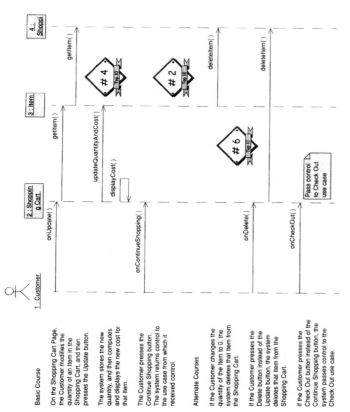

Basic Course

On the Shopping Cart Page, the Customer modifies the quantity of an Item in the Shopping Cart, and then presses the Update button.

The system stores the new quantity, and then computes and displays the new cost for that Item.

The Customer presses the Continue Shopping button. The system returns control to the use case from which it received control.

Alternate Courses

If the Customer changes the quantity of the Item to 0, the system deletes that Item from the Shopping Cart.

If the Customer presses the Delete button instead of the Update button, the system deletes that Item from the Shopping Cart.

If the Customer presses the Check Out button instead of the Continue Shopping button, the system passes control to the Check Out use case.

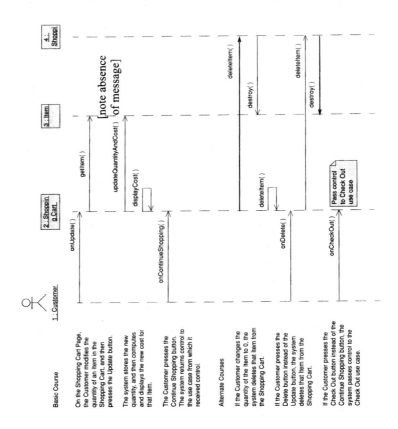

On the previous diagram:

- The second getItem method call clutters up the diagram.

- The Item object sends a deleteItem message to the Shopping Cart object.

- There are no destroy messages, which might indicate a hole in the designer's thinking, since the Items won't actually get deleted unless the system will be coded in a language, such as Java, that provides for automatic garbage collection).

Track Recent Orders

Basic Course

The system retrieves the Orders that the Customer has placed within the last 30 days, and displays these Orders on the Order Tracking Page. Each entry has the Order ID (in the form of a link), the Order date, the Order status, the Order recipient, and the Shipping Method by which the Order was shipped. The Customer clicks on a link. The system retrieves and displays the relevant contents of the Order, in view-only mode, on the Order Details Page. The Customer presses OK to return to the Order Tracking Page. Once the Customer has finished viewing Orders, he or she clicks the Account Maintenance link. The system returns control to the invoking use case.

Alternate Course

If the Customer has not placed any Orders within the last 30 days, the system displays a message to that effect on the Order Tracking Page.

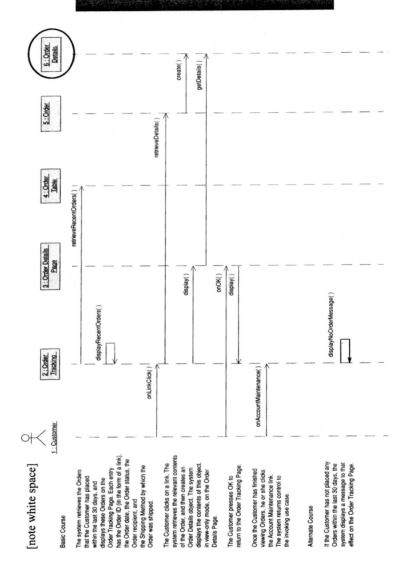

On the previous diagram:

- The use case test doesn't line up visually with the message arrows.

- There is no Order Details object, which would have been identified during robustness analysis, and thus the use case text is wrong, as well.

- The Order Table object invokes the displayNoOrderMessage method on the Order Tracking Page. It's a bad idea to have persistent database tables, or their proxy objects, invoking methods on the user interface.

Bringing the Pieces Together

Figures 7-3 to 7-5 together show a design-level class diagram for our Internet Bookstore. (The classes on the left side of Figure 7-3 match up with those on the right side of Figure 7-2. Figure 7-4 has a similar relationship with Figure 7-3.)

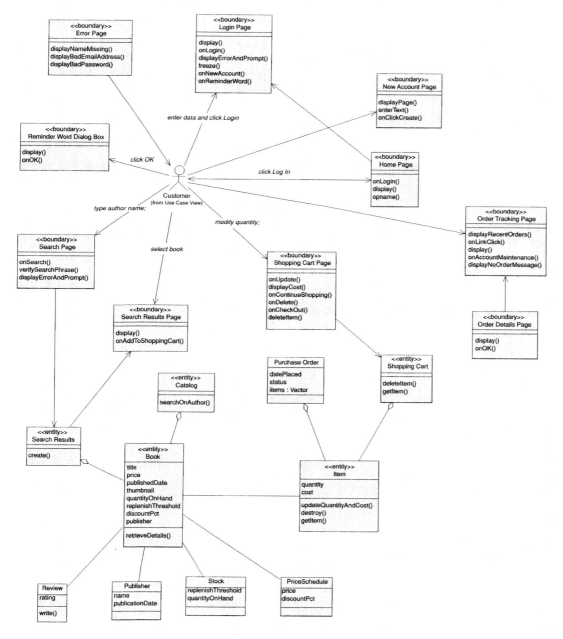

Figure 7-3: *Static Model for The Internet Bookstore (Part 1)*

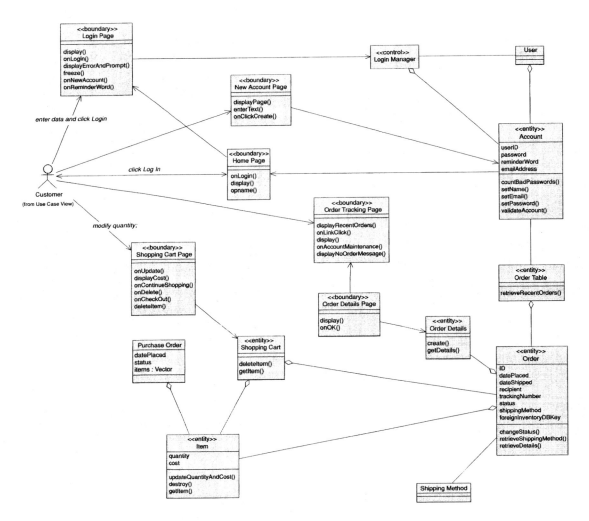

Figure 7-4: *Static Model for The Internet Bookstore (Part 2)*

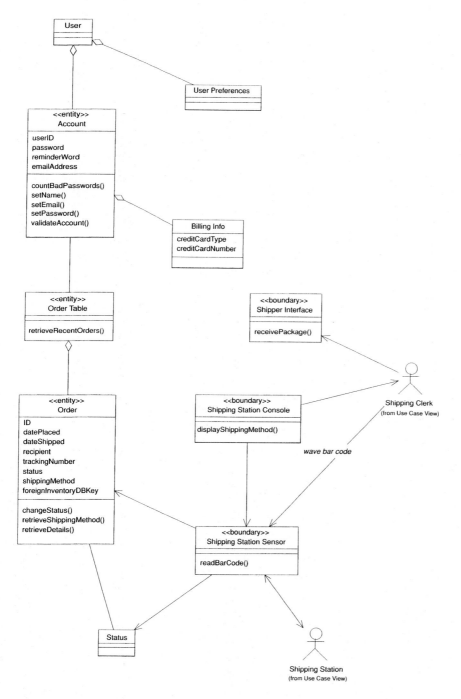

Figure 7-5: *Static Model for The Internet Bookstore (Part 3)*

Chapter 8

Critical Design Review

Critical design review (CDR) involves trying to ensure that the "how" of detailed design, as shown on sequence diagrams and associated class diagrams, matches up well with the "what" that the use cases specify, and that the detailed design is of sufficient depth to facilitate a relatively small and seamless leap into code. CDR also involves *reviewing the quality of your design* from a number of perspectives. These might include modularity, cohesiveness of your classes, coupling between objects, and a number of other metrics that we can lump together and call "OO goodness."

At this time, you might also be making sure that your design meets a set of internal design standards for your organization. Sometimes these standards might make use of design patterns. For example, there may be a project-wide decision to use factories to create instances of our objects. Or there might be standard access mechanisms for interfacing to an underlying relational database. The sequence diagrams, and the detailed class diagrams that go with them, should reflect the real software design, as the senior designers intend for it to be coded. We've made our best attempt to stabilize and validate our requirements and our technical architecture before we got here. CDR is the last stop before code, so at this point we're looking to nail down all of our remaining design issues. Figure 8-1 shows where we are.

The Key Elements of Critical Design Review

The first thing to keep in mind about CDR is that it should involve designers and developers more or less exclusively. We told you in Chapter 6 that preliminary design review (PDR) was the last chance for most of your customers to be involved on a hands-on basis. Unless you have customers who have significant expertise in detailed design, and who need to be involved in reviewing detailed designs (whether for technical or political reasons), you should, in effect, smile and say, "Thanks, we'll take it from here. Now that you've signed off on them twice, we're freezing the behavior descriptions until we get this stuff built. See you then, when you can test what we built against these behavior descriptions to verify that we built what you wanted."

• Allocate behavior. For each use case:

– Identify the messages that need to be passed between objects,
the objects, and the associated methods to be invoked.
Draw a sequence diagram with use case text running
down the left side and design information on the right.
Continue to update the class diagram with attributes
and operations as you find them.

– If you wish, show, on a collaboration diagram,
the key transactions between objects.

– If you wish, use a state diagram to show the real-time behavior.

• Finish the static model by adding detailed design
information (for instance, visibility values and patterns).

• Verify with your team that your design satisfies
all the requirements you've identified.

Milestone 3: Critical Design Review

Figure 8-1: *Critical Design Review and the ICONIX Process*

Before you commence CDR, you need to make sure that you have sequence diagrams for all of the use cases for which you're going to deliver code in the current release. Per our quote from Jacobson in Chapter 7, you can't be sure that you've found all of the responsibilities for each of your objects unless you've drawn sequence diagrams for *all* of your basic courses and *all* of your alternate courses for *all* of your use cases. Taken together, these diagrams form the core of your dynamic model, which should now show the behavior of your system at runtime, including *how* the system will accomplish that behavior, in great detail.

One key aspect of CDR involves performing a careful review of the matchups between each sentence of the use case text and the message(s) across from that text on the sequence diagram. The project team will have put a lot of effort into writing the use case text, and the user community should have signed off on the results. Also, *the robustness models will have demonstrated feasibility in the context of the object model*—in other words, we've found some objects that can work together to provide the required behavior. Now it's time to ensure that the "how" on the sequence diagram addresses the "what" specified by the use case.

It should be obvious which message or set of messages among the objects on the right-hand side of the diagram corresponds with each sentence of the use case, including the basic course and all alternate courses. Ensuring that the flow of messages corresponds well with the flow of the use case is critical in enforcing traceability of your design back to your customer-specified functional requirements. We recommend that senior designers perform this kind of review for more junior designers, and (think about it) that junior designers do the same for more senior designers.

The next thing to look for is continuity of messages. We told you in Chapter 7 that it's *essential* that you get the direction of message arrows right on sequence diagrams, that the flow of control needs to be explicit. It must be obvious at all times which object is in control. If you notice any leaps between objects that don't involve a message between those objects, you need to make sure the designers eliminate those leaps.

While designers are making behavior allocation decisions, they're making decisions that affect the quality of the classes in your design. Halbert and O'Brien defined four criteria of a good class, which designers should keep in mind at all times when deciding which methods belong with which objects on sequence diagrams:

- *Reusability.* The more general your objects and classes, the higher the probability that you'll be able to reuse those objects and classes for other projects. Ask yourself whether assigning a method to a class makes that class more or less reusable.

- *Applicability.* The concept of applicability is basically the same in the context of interaction modeling as it is for domain modeling and use case modeling. When you assign methods to the objects on your sequence diagrams, always ask yourself whether there seems to be a good fit between method and object, and also whether the task that the method performs is obviously relevant to the object.

- *Complexity.* Our first two criteria, reusability and applicability, are still somewhat theoretical. The subject of complexity is an indication that we're about to get serious about implementation issues. In essence, the issue here is whether it's easier to build a method in one or another object.

- *Implementation knowledge.* This criterion involves asking whether the implementation of the behavior depends on details internal to the associated method.

Applicability is probably the most important of these criteria. As you become experienced at OOD, you'll develop an intuitive sense of "fit." When this happens, you'll cut through the behavior allocation decisions on your sequence diagrams like a hot knife through butter.

Note that we learned about these criteria (and also the ones that follow) from Grady Booch's *Object-Oriented Analysis and Design with Applications* (Addison-Wesley, 1994).

Now is also a good time to think about your classes and ask yourself if they satisfy the following quality criteria:

- **Coupling** is a measure of the strength of a connection between two classes. You can improve the modularity of a system by designing it with *loose coupling* wherever possible. This translates into classes that are highly independent.

- **Cohesion** is a measure of how tightly connected the attributes and operations of a class are. It is desirable to strive for *high functional cohesion*, which occurs when the elements of each of your classes are working together to provide a clearly defined behavior (in other words, a single personality).

- **Sufficiency** is the condition in which a class encapsulates enough of the abstractions that your models present so that it offers something meaningful and efficient, with which other parts of the system can interact. The key question is whether the class covers all the relevant cases.

- **Completeness** is the condition in which a given class's interface captures all the relevant abstractions. So a complete class is one that is theoretically reusable in any number of contexts. Keep in mind, though, that you should be careful not to overdo your efforts in this direction—you might never get anything built.

- **Primitiveness** is the condition in which an operation can be efficiently built only if it has access to the material on which your models are built. The idea here is that you can design certain operations that you can use as building blocks for other operations as your design evolves.

Another criterion for a good sequence diagram is a sufficient amount of detail. Sequence diagrams serve as the last stop before coding and as such need to show the real design in full detail. You shouldn't consider this part of the project done until *all* the methods from your sequence diagrams are assigned to classes within your static model, and you've factored in "Booch stuff," such as abstract and parameterized classes, friend relationships, and composition. (Booch stuff is especially important if you're going to code in C++.) You also need to address issues related to things such as persistent storage and the distribution of objects across your system.

By the way, if you are building in C++ and you want to learn more about Booch stuff, we recommend (in addition to the Booch book) Robert Martin's book *Designing Object Oriented C++ Applications Using the Booch Method* (Prentice Hall, 1995). Bob wrote this book before he started teaching XP. One of our favorite quotes is from page 43, where he writes, under the heading "Why Is This Better Than Writing Code?", the following:

> Why should you go to all the trouble of drawing these diagrams, when the code explains things just as well, if not better? For problems as simple as the one above, you shouldn't. Diagramming such simple models is an exercise in futility and pedantry. I have done it here only to demonstrate the mechanics of the diagrams, not their intended use. The advantage to using the diagrams will become more apparent as we go on to study more and more complex examples. The diagrams allow us to visualize, on one page, concepts that might take dozens of pages of C++ code to express. They also allow us to quickly play with these concepts and communicate them to others. Moreover, as we just saw in the discussion of the uses relationships, these diagrams allow us to visualize physical compiler dependencies as well as logic and algorithmic concepts, so that we can make a full spectrum of decisions about the static and dynamic structure of an application. Not only can we examine the logical consistency of the design, but we can also probe how well the design will fit into our development environment.

Although Bob is now off preaching the XP gospel, we think he had this about right the first time through.

A surefire sign of a "generic" sequence diagram is the absence of implementation details, such as those having to do with distribution. If you're using a technology such as DCOM or EJB, your sequence diagrams should reflect how you're using specific elements of that technology. Remember: You can't effectively build code from a detailed design if the connection between the design and the implementation environment isn't obvious.

Looking in another direction: As you're reviewing the interactions among the various objects, you may decide that one or more well-established design patterns would fit in nicely. You might choose to use the *Factory Method* pattern, which lets a class defer instantiation to subclasses, or *Iterator*, which lets a client traverse a list in various ways, without needing to know how that list has been implemented. See *Design Patterns* (Erich Gamma, Richard Helm, Ralph Johnson, and John Vlissides: Addison-Wesley, 1995) for more information about these and other design patterns. Or perhaps you might develop new patterns to establish a standardized approach to design problems that appear across multiple use cases. *This* is the time to review all of these decisions and make sure you're comfortable with them, because soon these design decisions will be reflected in code.

We introduced the concept of technical architecture in Chapter 6 as being the set of basic decisions you need to make about what technologies you're going to use in implementing the system: the programming language, how you're going to build and distribute software components, and so forth. We told you that the decisions you make about your technical architecture need to be reflected on your robustness diagrams. During CDR, you need to validate the detailed design as it reflects and expands upon that technical architecture. Where one of the goals of PDR is to ensure the "do-ability" of the architecture, here you're looking to actually build that architecture to implement your scenarios.

The Top 10 CDR Errors

The flip side of the principles we just discussed takes the form of a number of common errors that our students make when they're doing critical design review for their projects. Our "Top 10" list follows.

Invite nontechnical customers to the design review.

Sequence diagrams are generally full of details that most likely won't mean much to any but the most technically aware customers. They exist to be used by designers and developers. Thus, CDR sessions should include those people involved in detailed design and development decisions, and no one else.

Don't check the use case text carefully against the body of the sequence diagram.

A reviewer should be able to see easily the visual trace between a sentence of use case text and a message, or set of messages, that describe that behavior in terms of object interactions. The right-hand side of the diagram should also account for all of the use case's alternate courses of action in ways that are clear to the reader. If this doesn't hold true, it's possible that the designer who did the diagram hasn't fully addressed the requirements expressed by the given use case.

Don't check the origin and destination of every message arrow on every sequence diagram carefully.

It's essential that a sequence diagram show which object is in control at all times. If there are discontinuities, there will be problems with the code if someone tries to build it based on the diagram.

Don't think through the Halbert/O'Brien criteria as you review your sequence diagrams.

You should look for a high degree of reusability of objects across your sequence diagrams, and a high level of applicability of methods within each object. You should also look to keep the complexity level, and the level of implementation specificity, low within methods and within objects as a whole. Working to meet these quality criteria will give you a healthy foundation for a robust object-oriented design.

Don't review your static models for "quality class" criteria.

One of the best sources of guidance for making good behavior allocation decisions is responsibility-driven design. As we explained in Chapter 7, a class should have a single "personality," and you should avoid "schizophrenic" objects. This means that a class should be focused on a strongly related set of behaviors that have minimal dependencies on other classes. The most important of the "quality class" criteria presented earlier in this chapter are high cohesion and loose coupling; single-personality classes are essential to achieving these goals. To expand on this, let's turn to Rebecca Wirfs-Brock (*Designing Object-Oriented Software*, Prentice Hall, 1990): "Responsibilities are meant to convey a sense of the purpose of an object and its place in the system. The responsibilities of an object are all the services it provides for all the contracts it supports. When we assign responsibilities to a class we are stating that each and every instance of that class will have those responsibilities, whether there is just one instance or many." *Make sure, if at all possible, that somebody who's read the Wirfs-Brock book—and understood it—participates in your critical design review.*

Don't worry about the "plumbing"; it will take care of itself.

The sequence diagrams serve as the last stop before coding and as such need to show the real design in full detail. This includes details about persistent storage (to which database tables are you going to map the various objects?) and distribution (on which layer or tier will each object reside?).

Don't consider whether design patterns would be of any use in your design.

Design patterns can provide you with a great deal of leverage with regard to the reusability and maintainability of your design. The more patterns you discover and reuse across your sequence diagrams, the greater the momentum you can build as you push toward code, and the more time you'll have to focus on the hard decisions that don't lend themselves to patternizing.

Show "generic" sequence diagrams that disregard implementation technology such as DCOM or EJBs.

As we said earlier in this chapter, sequence diagrams are the last step before code within the ICONIX process. You should be working to minimize the size of the gap that you have to cross between detailed design and implementation by adding a reasonable amount of detail about the technology you're using to build the system.

Don't review sequence diagrams for every scenario that will be built in the current release.

If you don't have, or don't go through, sequence diagrams for one or more of your use cases, or if any of your diagrams don't show both the basic course *and* all alternate courses for the given use case, there's a good chance that you will miss some behavior that one or more objects needs to perform, make some decisions about behavior allocation that aren't optimal, or both.

\Don't worry about the details of your design before you jump into code. Just assume that refactoring the code will fix everything.

Refactoring is defined, in Martin Fowler's book *Refactoring* (Addison-Wesley, 2000) as "the process of changing a software system in such a way that it does not alter the external behavior of the code yet improves its internal structure." This sounds like an excellent technique for optimizing code. However, XPers also rely heavily on the likes of this, from *Extreme Programming Installed* (Ron Jeffries, Ann Anderson, and Chet Hendrickson; Addison-Wesley, 2001): "[W]hen the design wants to change, as it will, change it." People who discover—and change—the design while they're coding are probably not going to build systems as robust as those built by people who spend a sufficient amount of time completing, and reviewing, the design before coding begins, because *you lose the global view of the design when you're focused on coding one small piece of it.* Refactoring won't guarantee that everything comes out right if you've merrily skipped past analysis and design—and it certainly won't guarantee that you're building the right system (that is, the one that meets your users' requirements).

Trying to design and code at the same time is like playing chess on the Internet while you're doing your calculus homework. You might be thinking, "Wow, I must be really smart to be able to do this!" to yourself, but if you're like most people, both your chess rating and your math grade would probably improve if you undertook these two mentally demanding tasks separately. (We used to know a guy who wore a T-shirt that said "The clever programmer outsmarts himself again.")

Both design and coding (and for that matter, analysis) are skills in their own right, and there are numerous aspects that must be kept track of at each phase of development. We're about at the end of the book, so we'd like to leave you with this final thought: All humans are fallible, and one of the best ways to reduce error rates is to focus on one thing at a time. "One thing at a time" is one of the central themes that's woven through the ICONIX Process. Even if you take nothing else from this book, we think you'll be more successful if you try to at least keep that simple fact in mind.

Appendix

This Appendix contains a report that summarizes the Rational Rose model for our Internet Bookstore. This report includes the following:

- the class diagram at the end of Chapter 2
- the "good" text for all of the use cases represented in Chapter 3
- the use case diagram at the end of Chapter 3
- all of the "good" robustness diagrams from Chapter 5
- the class diagram at the end of Chapter 5
- all of the "good" sequence diagrams from Chapter 7
- the class diagrams at the end of Chapter 7

Rational Rose Model Report

Rose Use Case Model

Use Case Documentation

USE CASE VIEW REPORT

Use Case View

Use Case Diagram - Main

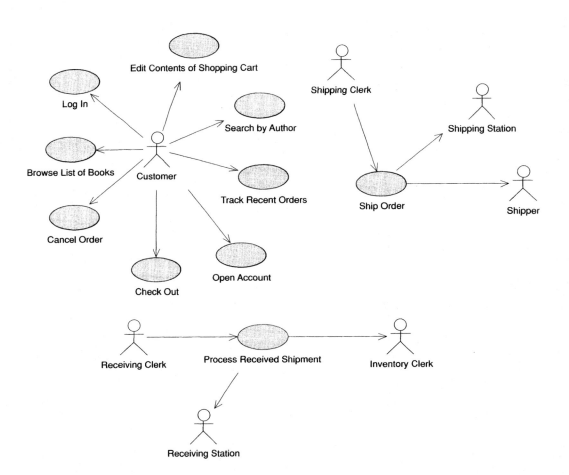

Class Diagram - Domain Model

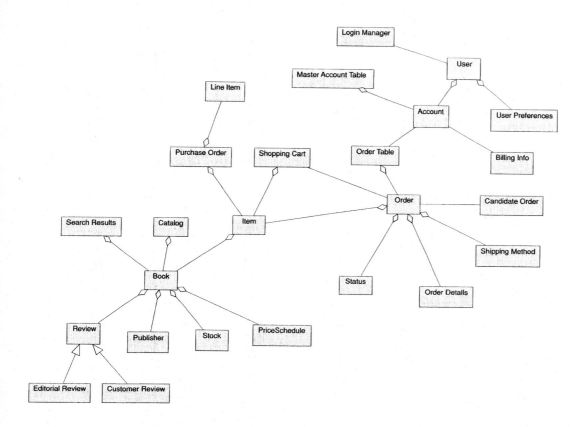

Class Diagram - Domain Model with Attributes

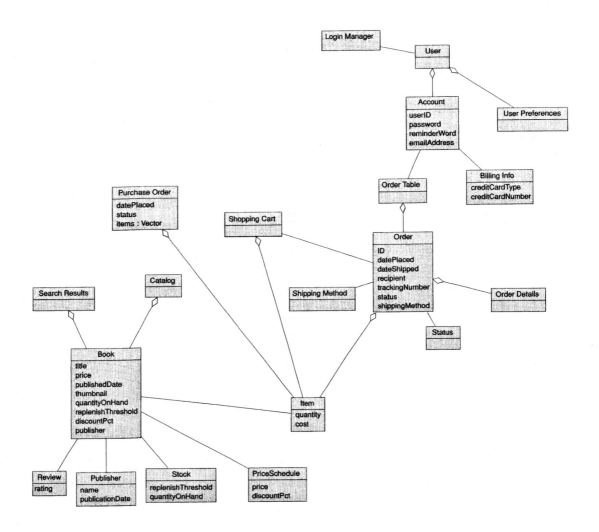

Class Diagram - Static Model (Part One)

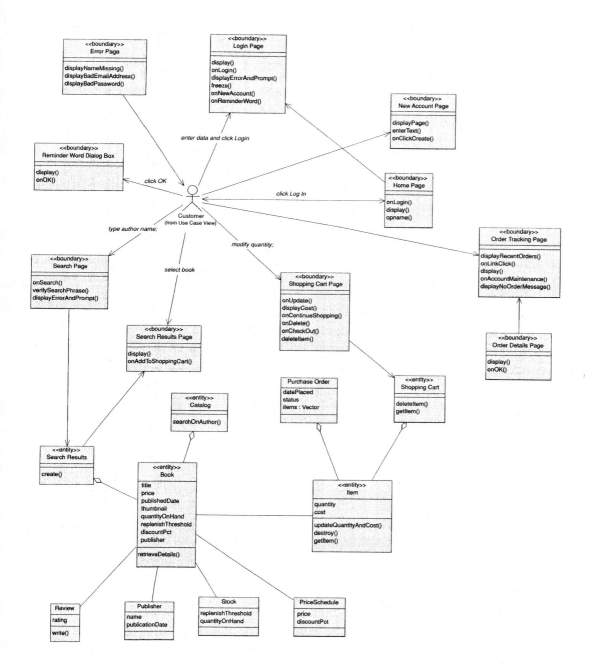

Class Diagram - Static Model (Part Two)

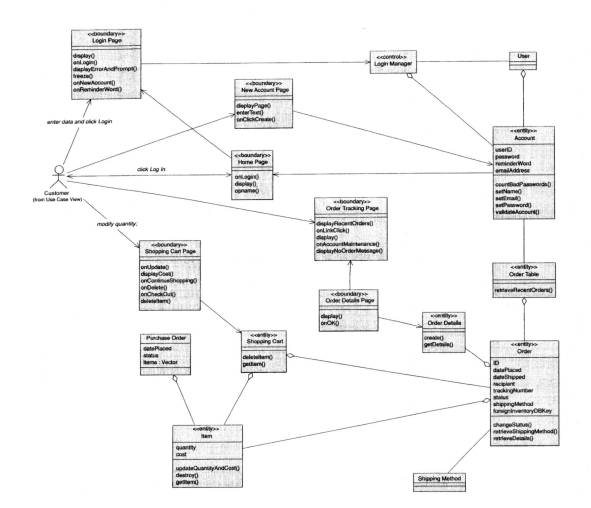

Class Diagram - Static Model (Part Three)

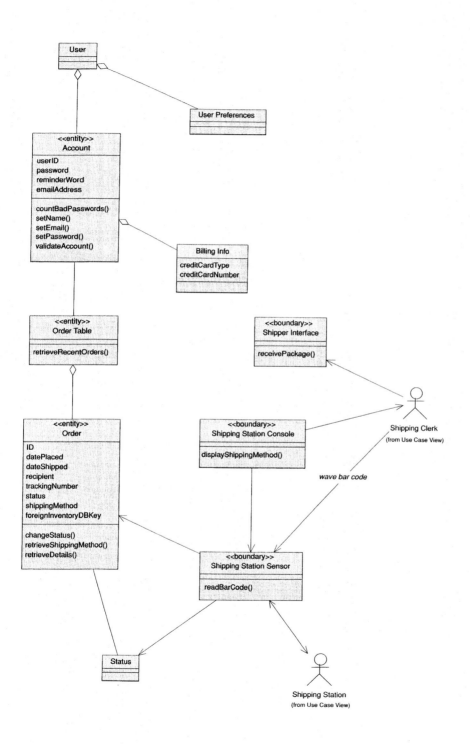

Actor - Customer

Actor - Shipping Clerk

Actor - Shipper

Actor - Receiving Clerk

Actor - Inventory Clerk

Actor - Shipping Station

Actor - Receiving Station

Use Case – Browse List of Books

Documentation:

Basic Course

The Customer clicks on a Category on the Browse Books Page. The system displays the subcategories within that Category. This process continues until there are no more subcategories, at which point the system displays the Books in the lowest subcategory. The Customer clicks on the thumbnail for a Book. The system invokes the Display Book Details use case.

Alternate Course

If the system does not find any Books contained within a given Category, it displays a message to that effect and prompts the Customer to select a different Category.

List of Associations

Customer Communicates with Browse List of Books

Use Case - Cancel Order

Documentation:

Basic Course

The system ensures that the Order is cancellable (in other words, that its status isn't "shipping" or "shipped"). Then the system displays the relevant information for the Order on the Cancel Order Page, including its contents and the shipping address. The Customer presses the Confirm Cancel button. The system marks the Order status as "deleted" and then invokes the Return Items to Inventory use case.

Alternate Course

If the status of the Order is "shipping" or "shipped," the system displays a message indicating that it's too late for the Customer to cancel the order.

List of Associations

Search Results Page Communicates with Cancel Order

Use Case – Check Out

Documentation:

Basic Course

The system creates a Candidate Order object that contains the contents of the Customer's Shopping Cart. Then the system retrieves the Shipping Addresses associated with the Customer's Account and displays these addresses on the Shipping Address Page.

The Customer selects an address and then presses the Use This Address button. The system associates the given Shipping Address with the Candidate Order. Then the system displays the available Shipping Methods on the Shipping Method Page.

The Customer selects a shipping method and then presses the Use This Shipping Method button. The system associates the given Shipping Method with the Candidate Order. Then the system displays the contents of the Billing Info objects associated with the Customer's Account, on the Billing Information Page.

The Customer selects a billing method and presses the Use This Billing Information button. The system associates the given Billing Info object with the Candidate Order. Then the system displays the Confirm Order Page.

The Customer presses the Confirm Order button. The system converts the Candidate Order to an Order and destroys the Shopping Cart. Then the system returns control to the use case from which this use case received control.

Alternate Courses

If the Customer has not already logged in, the system invokes the Log In use case.

If the system does not find any Shipping Addresses, it invokes the Create Shipping Address use case.

If the system does not find any Billing Info objects, it invokes the Define Billing Information use case.

If the Customer presses the Cancel Order button at any time, the system destroys the Candidate Order and returns control to the use case from which this use case received control.

List of Associations

Customer Communicates with Check Out
Shopping Cart Page Communicates with Check Out

Use Case - Edit Contents of Shopping Cart

Documentation:

Basic Course

On the Shopping Cart Page, the Customer modifies the quantity of an Item in the Shopping Cart and then presses the Update button. The system stores the new quantity and then computes and displays the new cost for that Item.

The Customer presses the Continue Shopping button. The system returns control to the use case from which it received control.

Alternate Courses

If the Customer changes the quantity of the Item to 0, the system deletes that Item from the Shopping Cart.

If the Customer presses the Delete button instead of the Update button, the system deletes that Item from the Shopping Cart.

If the Customer presses the Check Out button instead of the Continue Shopping button, the system passes control to the Check Out use case.

List of Associations

Customer Communicates with Edit Contents of Shopping Cart

Class Diagram - Edit Contents of Shopping Cart Robustness

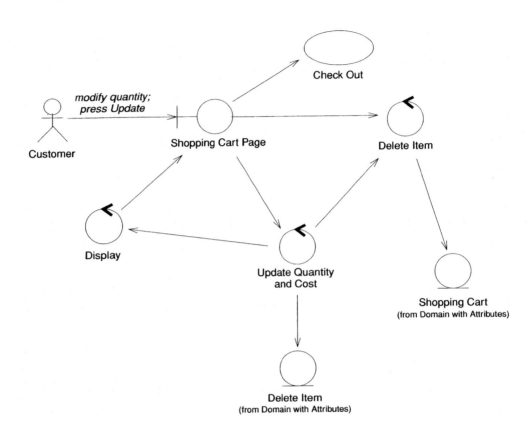

Interaction Diagram - Edit Contents of Shopping Cart Sequence

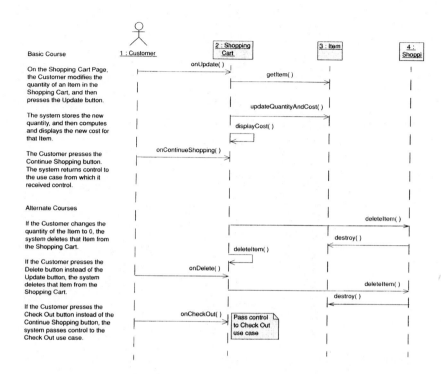

Basic Course

On the Shopping Cart Page, the Customer modifies the quantity of an Item in the Shopping Cart, and then presses the Update button.

The system stores the new quantity, and then computes and displays the new cost for that Item.

The Customer presses the Continue Shopping button. The system returns control to the use case from which it received control.

Alternate Courses

If the Customer changes the quantity of the Item to 0, the system deletes that Item from the Shopping Cart.

If the Customer presses the Delete button instead of the Update button, the system deletes that Item from the Shopping Cart.

If the Customer presses the Check Out button instead of the Continue Shopping button, the system passes control to the Check Out use case.

Use Case - Log In

Documentation:

Basic Course

The Customer clicks the Log In button on the Home Page. The system displays the Login Page. The Customer enters his or her user ID and password and then clicks the Log In button.

The system validates the login information against the persistent Account data and then returns the Customer to the Home Page.

Alternate Courses

If the Customer clicks the New Account button on the Login Page, the system invokes the Open Account use case.

If the Customer clicks the Reminder Word button on the Login Page, the system displays the reminder word stored for that Customer, in a separate dialog box. When the Customer clicks the OK button, the system returns the Customer to the Login Page.

If the Customer enters a user ID that the system does not recognize, the system displays a message to that effect and prompts the Customer to either enter a different ID or click the New Account button.

If the Customer enters an incorrect password, the system displays a message to that effect and prompts the Customer to reenter his or her password.

If the Customer enters an incorrect password three times, the system displays a page telling the Customer that he or she should contact customer service and also freezes the Login Page.

List of Associations

Customer Communicates with Log In

Class Diagram - Log In Robustness

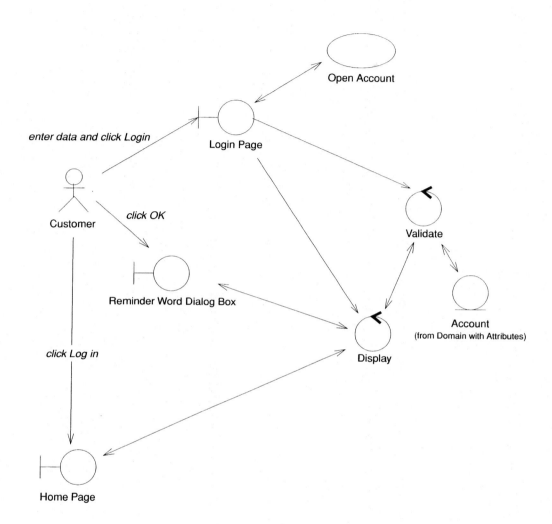

Interaction Diagram - Log In Sequence

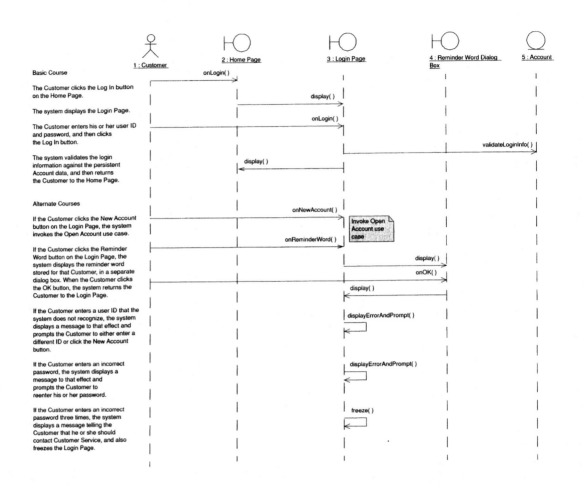

Basic Course

The Customer clicks the Log In button on the Home Page.

The system displays the Login Page.

The Customer enters his or her user ID and password, and then clicks the Log In button.

The system validates the login information against the persistent Account data, and then returns the Customer to the Home Page.

Alternate Courses

If the Customer clicks the New Account button on the Login Page, the system invokes the Open Account use case.

If the Customer clicks the Reminder Word button on the Login Page, the system displays the reminder word stored for that Customer, in a separate dialog box. When the Customer clicks the OK button, the system returns the Customer to the Login Page.

If the Customer enters a user ID that the system does not recognize, the system displays a message to that effect and prompts the Customer to either enter a different ID or click the New Account button.

If the Customer enters an incorrect password, the system displays a message to that effect and prompts the Customer to reenter his or her password.

If the Customer enters an incorrect password three times, the system displays a message telling the Customer that he or she should contact Customer Service, and also freezes the Login Page.

Use Case - Open Account

Documentation:

Basic Course

The Customer types his or her name, an e-mail address, and a password (twice), and then presses the Create Account button. The system ensures that the Customer has provided valid data and then adds an Account to the Master Account Table using that data. Then the system returns the Customer to the Home Page.

Alternate Courses

If the Customer did not provide a name, the system displays an error message to that effect and prompts the Customer to type a name.

If the Customer provided an email address that's not in the correct form, the system displays an error message to that effect and prompts the Customer to type a different address.

If the Customer provided a password that is too short, the system displays an error message to that effect and prompts the Customer to type a longer password.

If the Customer did not type the same password twice, the system displays an error message to that effect and prompts the Customer to type the password correctly the second time.

If the account is already in the Master Account Table, the system tells the Customer.

List of Associations

Customer Communicates with Open Account
Login Page Communicates with Open Account
Open Account Communicates with Login Page

Use Case - Process Received Shipment

Documentation:

Basic Course

The Receiving Clerk ensures that the Line Items listed on the Purchase Order match the physical items. The Clerk waves the bar code on the packing slip under the sensor at the receiving station.

The system changes the status of the Purchase Order to "fulfilled" and updates the quantity on hand values for the various Books. The Clerk hands the Books off to the Inventory Clerk.

Alternate Course

If the Receiving Clerk finds a mismatch between the Purchase Order and the physical items, the Clerk stops processing of the shipment until he or she is able to make a match.

List of Associations

Receiving Clerk Communicates with Process Received Shipment
Process Received Shipment Communicates with Inventory Clerk
Process Received Shipment Communicates with Receiving Station

Use Case – Search by Author

Documentation:

Basic Course

The Customer types the name of an Author on the Search Page and presses the Search button. The system ensures that the Customer typed a search phrase and then searches the Catalog and retrieves all of the Books with which that Author is associated.

The system retrieves the important details about each Book and creates a Search Results object with that information. Then the system displays the list of Books on the Search Results Page, with the Books listed in reverse chronological order by publication date. Each entry has a thumbnail of the Book's cover, the Book's title and authors, the average Rating, and an Add to Shopping Cart button.

The Customer presses the Add to Shopping Cart button for a particular Book. The system passes control to the Add Item to Shopping Cart use case.

Alternate Courses

If the Customer did not type a search phrase before pressing the Search button, the system displays an error message to that effect and prompts the Customer to type a search phrase.

If the system was unable to find any Books associated with the Author that the Customer specified, the system displays a message to that effect and prompts the Customer to perform a different search.

If the Customer leaves the page in a way other than by pressing an Add to Shopping Cart button, the system returns control to the use case from which this use case received control.

List of Associations

Customer Communicates with Search by Author

Class Diagram - Search by Author Robustness

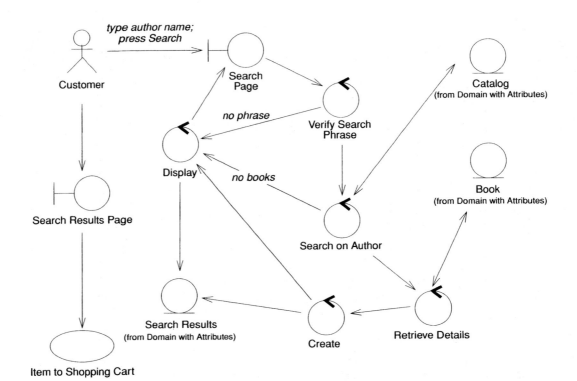

Interaction Diagram – Search by Author Sequence

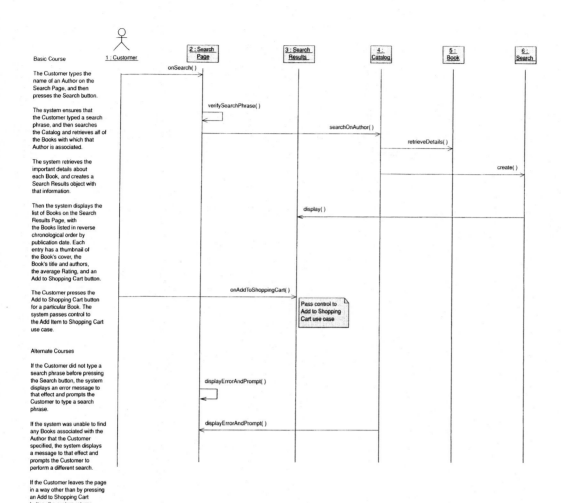

Basic Course

The Customer types the name of an Author on the Search Page, and then presses the Search button.

The system ensures that the Customer typed a search phrase, and then searches the Catalog and retrieves all of the Books with which that Author is associated.

The system retrieves the important details about each Book, and creates a Search Results object with that information.

Then the system displays the list of Books on the Search Results Page, with the Books listed in reverse chronological order by publication date. Each entry has a thumbnail of the Book's cover, the Book's title and authors, the average Rating, and an Add to Shopping Cart button.

The Customer presses the Add to Shopping Cart button for a particular Book. The system passes control to the Add Item to Shopping Cart use case.

Alternate Courses

If the Customer did not type a search phrase before pressing the Search button, the system displays an error message to that effect and prompts the Customer to type a search phrase.

If the system was unable to find any Books associated with the Author that the Customer specified, the system displays a message to that effect and prompts the Customer to perform a different search.

If the Customer leaves the page in a way other than by pressing an Add to Shopping Cart button, the system returns control to the use case from which this use case received control.

Use Case - Ship Order

Documentation:

Basic Course

The Shipping Clerk ensures that the Items listed on the packing slip for the Order match the physical items. The Clerk waves the bar code on the packing slip under the sensor at the shipping station.

The system changes the status of the Order to "shipping." Then the system retrieves the Shipping Method that the Customer specified for this Order and displays it on the Shipping Station Console.

The Clerk weighs the set of physical items. The Clerk packages the Items. The Clerk attaches a manifest appropriate for the given shipping method. The Clerk waves the bar code on the manifest under the sensor. The Clerk sends the package out via the associated Shipper.

Alternate Course

If the Shipping Clerk finds a mismatch between the Order and the physical items, the Clerk stops processing of the Order until he or she is able to make a match.

List of Associations

Shipping Clerk Communicates with Ship Order
Ship Order Communicates with Shipper
Ship Order Communicates with Shipping Station

Class Diagram - Ship Order Robustness

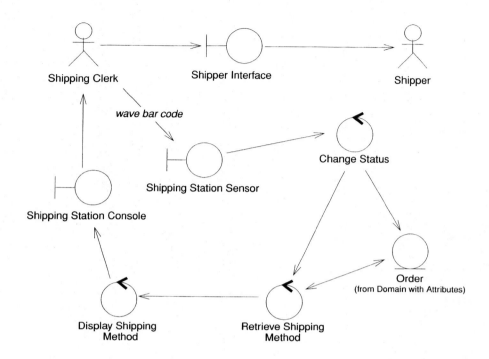

Interaction Diagram - Ship Order Sequence

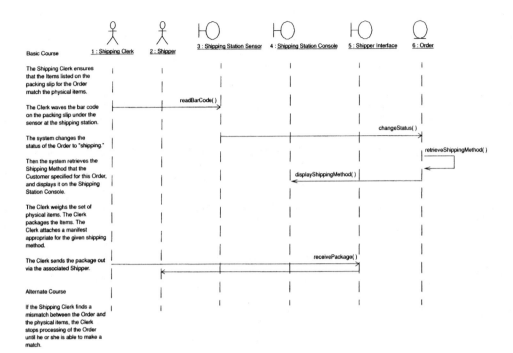

Basic Course

1 : Shipping Clerk **2 : Shipper** **3 : Shipping Station Sensor** **4 : Shipping Station Console** **5 : Shipper Interface** **6 : Order**

The Shipping Clerk ensures that the Items listed on the packing slip for the Order match the physical items.

The Clerk waves the bar code on the packing slip under the sensor at the shipping station.

readBarCode( )

changeStatus( )

The system changes the status of the Order to "shipping."

retrieveShippingMethod( )

Then the system retrieves the Shipping Method that the Customer specified for this Order, and displays it on the Shipping Station Console.

displayShippingMethod( )

The Clerk weighs the set of physical items. The Clerk packages the Items. The Clerk attaches a manifest appropriate for the given shipping method.

The Clerk sends the package out via the associated Shipper.

receivePackage( )

Alternate Course

If the Shipping Clerk finds a mismatch between the Order and the physical items, the Clerk stops processing of the Order until he or she is able to make a match.

Use Case – Track Recent Orders

Documentation:

Basic Course

The system retrieves the Orders that the Customer has placed within the last 30 days and displays these Orders on the Order Tracking Page. Each entry has the Order ID (in the form of a link), the Order date, the Order status, the Order recipient, and the Shipping Method by which the Order was shipped.

The Customer clicks on a link. The system retrieves the relevant contents of the Order and then displays this information, in view-only mode, on the Order Details Page. The Customer presses OK to return to the Order Tracking Page.

Once the Customer has finished viewing Orders, he or she clicks the Account Mainte-nance link on the Order Tracking Page. The system returns control to the invoking use case.

Alternate Course

If the Customer has not placed any Orders within the last 30 days, the system displays a message to that effect on the Order Tracking Page.

List of Associations

Customer Communicates with Track Recent Orders

Class Diagram - Track Recent Orders Robustness

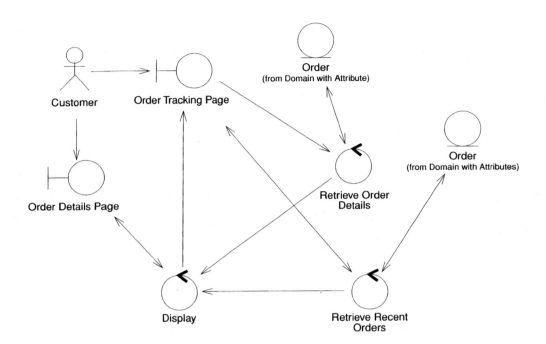

Interaction Diagram - Track Recent Orders Sequence

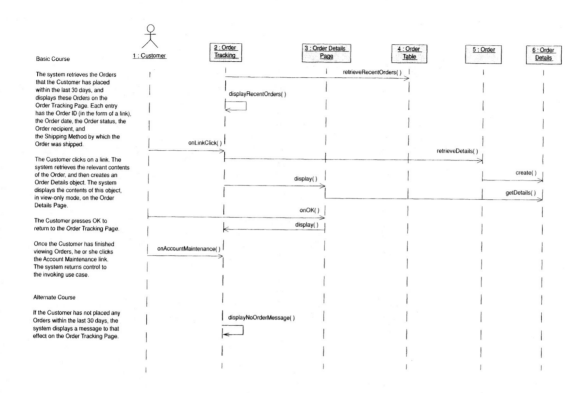

Basic Course

The system retrieves the Orders that the Customer has placed within the last 30 days, and displays these Orders on the Order Tracking Page. Each entry has the Order ID (in the form of a link), the Order date, the Order status, the Order recipient, and the Shipping Method by which the Order was shipped.

The Customer clicks on a link. The system retrieves the relevant contents of the Order, and then creates an Order Details object. The system displays the contents of this object, in view-only mode, on the Order Details Page.

The Customer presses OK to return to the Order Tracking Page.

Once the Customer has finished viewing Orders, he or she clicks the Account Maintenance link. The system returns control to the invoking use case.

Alternate Course

If the Customer has not placed any Orders within the last 30 days, the system displays a message to that effect on the Order Tracking Page.

TOTALS:

2 Packages
10 Use Cases

USE CASE PACKAGE STRUCTURE

Use Case View

Bibliography

Grady Booch: *Object-Oriented Analysis and Design with Applications, Second Edition*. Addison-Wesley, 1994.

Grady Booch, James Rumbaugh, and Ivar Jacobson: *The Unified Modeling Language User Guide*. Addison Wesley Longman, 1999.

Peter DeGrace and Leslie Hulet Stahl: *The Olduvai Imperative*. Prentice Hall, 1993.

Tom DeMarco: *Structured Analysis and System Specification*. Prentice Hall, 1985.

Kurt Derr: *Applying OMT*. SIGS Books, 1995.

Bruce Powel Douglass: *Real-Time UML: Developing Efficient Objects for Embedded Systems*. Addison Wesley Longman, 1998.

Martin Fowler: *Refactoring*. Addison-Wesley, 2000.

Erich Gamma, Richard Helm, Ralph Johnson, and John Vlissides [Gang of Four]: *Design Patterns: Elements of Reusable Object-Oriented Software*. Addison-Wesley, 1995.

Maurice Howard Halstead: *Elements of Software Science*. 1977. Out of print.

Ivar Jacobson, Magnus Christerson, Patrick Jonsson, and Gunnar Overgaard: *Object-Oriented Software Engineering: A Use Case Driven Approach*. Addison-Wesley, 1992.

Ivar Jacobson, Maria Ericsson, and Agneta Jacobson: *The Object Advantage: Business Process Reengineering with Object Technology*. Addison-Wesley, 1995.

Ron Jeffries, Ann Anderson, and Chet Hendrickson: *Extreme Programming Installed*. Addison-Wesley, 2001.

Chris Kemerer: *Software Project Management: Readings and Cases*. Richard D. Irwin, 1996.

Robert Cecil Martin: *Designing Object-Oriented C++ Applications Using the Booch Method*. Prentice Hall, 1995.

Doug Rosenberg: "Applying O-O Methods to Interactive Multimedia Projects," *OBJECT*, June 1995.

Doug Rosenberg: *Inside the ICONIX Process* (CD-ROM; ICONIX, 2001).

Doug Rosenberg: *Mastering UML with Rational Rose* (CD-ROM; ICONIX, 1997).

Doug Rosenberg: "Modeling Client/Server Systems," *OBJECT*, March 1994.

Doug Rosenberg: *An Object Methodology Overview* (CD-ROM; ICONIX, 1994).

Doug Rosenberg: *Rational Rose 98 for Power Users* (CD-ROM; ICONIX, 1998).

Doug Rosenberg: "UML Applied: Nine Tips to Incorporating UML Into Your Project," *Software Development*, March 1998.

Doug Rosenberg: *A Unified Object Modeling Approach* (2 CD-ROM set; ICONIX, 1996).

Doug Rosenberg: "Using the Object Modeling Technique with Objectory for Client/Server Development," *OBJECT*, November 1993.

Doug Rosenberg: "Validating the Design of Client/Server Systems," *OBJECT*, July 1994.

Doug Rosenberg and Kendall Scott: "Optimizing Rose 98 to Support Use Case Driven Object Modeling." Available at **http://www.rosearchitect.com/archives/9810/online.shtml**.

Doug Rosenberg and Kendall Scott: *Use Case Driven Object Modeling with UML: A Practical Approach*. Addison Wesley Longman, 1999.

James Rumbaugh, Michael Blaha, William Premerlani, Frederick Eddy, and William Lorenzen: *Object-Oriented Modeling and Design*. Prentice Hall, 1991.

William Shakespeare: *Much Ado About Nothing*. Public domain.

Rebecca Wirfs-Brock, Brian Wilkerson, and Lauren Wiener: *Designing Object-Oriented Software*. Prentice Hall, 1990.

Index

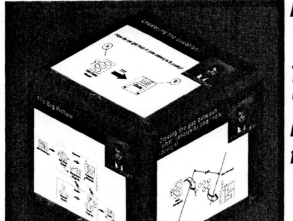

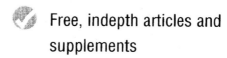
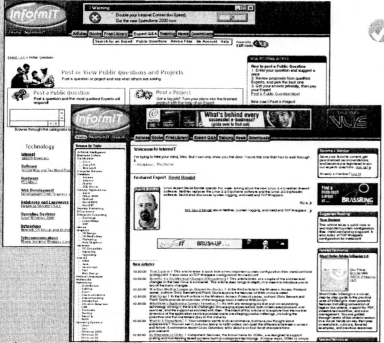

Register Your Book

at www.aw.com/cseng/register

You may be eligible to receive:
- Advance notice of forthcoming editions of the book
- Related book recommendations
- Chapter excerpts and supplements of forthcoming titles
- Information about special contests and promotions throughout the year
- Notices and reminders about author appearances, tradeshows, and online chats with special guests

Contact us

If you are interested in writing a book or reviewing manuscripts prior to publication, please write to us at:

Editorial Department
Addison-Wesley Professional
75 Arlington Street, Suite 300
Boston, MA 02116 USA
Email: AWPro@aw.com

Visit us on the Web: http://www.aw.com/cseng